Developing SSRS Reports for Dynamics AX

A step-by-step guide to Microsoft Dynamics AX 2012 report development using real-world scenarios

Mukesh Hirwani

[PACKT] enterprise

PUBLISHING

professional expertise distilled

BIRMINGHAM - MUMBAI

Developing SSRS Reports for Dynamics AX

First published: September 2013

Production Reference: 2190913

Published by Packt Publishing Ltd.
Livery Place
35 Livery Street
Birmingham B3 2PB, UK.
ISBN 978-1-78217-774-6

www.packtpub.com

Cover Image by Jarek Blaminsky (milak6@wp.pl)

Credits

Author

Mukesh Hirwani

Reviewers

Manoj Nuthakki

Umesh Pandit

Acquisition Editor

Joanne Fitzpatrick

Commissioning Editor

Amit Ghodake

Technical Editors

Abhishek Banthia

Larissa Pinto

Aman Preet Singh

Project Coordinator

Michelle Quadros

Proofreader

Linda Morris

Indexer

Hemangini Bari

Graphics

Ronak Dhruv

Production Coordinator

Kyle Albuquerque

Cover Work

Kyle Albuquerque

About the Author

Mukesh Hirwani is currently working as a Technical Solution Architect with Microsoft Dynamics Gold Partner. The company provides specialized solutions to the family of Microsoft Dynamics Partners/Resellers/Customers.

Mukesh started his career back in the year 2008 parallel to his Post-graduation (Master of Science Studies in Software Engineering from the Birla Institute of Technology and Science). Since then, he has been a recognized Microsoft Certified Professional for AX in all the major areas: Development, Configuration and Installation, Integration, Financials, Projects, Customer Relationship Management, Human Resources, and Trade and Logistics. He has also been delivering trainings for AX Technical Track.

From 2008 to 2013, Mukesh has participated in over 12 Microsoft Dynamics AX implementations. He has handled a wide range of development, consulting, and leading roles, while always maintaining a significant role as an Enterprise Application Developer.

In the early days of the year 2013, Mukesh has worked with Microsoft for AX 2012 R2 learning material preparation.

First of all, I would like to thank my parents, specially my Mom, Dad, and Brother for their continuous support, guidance, and understanding, during the long hours I spent on this book. I would also like to thank my fiancé Arti, for her patience and support during the time I have been writing this book.

Secondly, I would like to thank the reviewer Manoj, and my colleagues who have provided a number of valuable suggestions during material preparation for this book.

And lastly, special thanks to the Packt Publishing team, who provided me with a chance to author this book.

About the Reviewers

Manoj Nuthakki is the Founder and CEO of 42Hertz INC, an enterprise IT solutions provider. The company offers business and technology consulting, systems integration, application services, custom software development, and support services across business verticals such as Enterprise Architecture Consulting, Enterprise Resource Planning, and Customer Relationship Management. 42Hertz specializes in providing a complete range of services for popular platforms like Microsoft Dynamics AX, Microsoft Dynamics CRM, Microsoft SharePoint, and SQL BI.

Manoj has over 10 years of experience in Microsoft Dynamics AX in software development, product, and project management. He has authored the Microsoft courseware and is a Microsoft Certified Trainer for Microsoft Dynamics AX courses. He has presented at several technical conferences including Convergence, TechReady, and many AX Readiness events. He regularly conducts webinars on advanced topics in BI. Manoj also works independently in the capacity of a Senior Technical Solution Architect and Advisor to partners and customers implementing Microsoft Dynamics AX.

Before founding 42Hertz, Manoj worked as a Senior Program Manager with the Dynamics AX product team at Microsoft, Redmond. During his tenure at Microsoft, he led efforts on several reporting and analytics features of the product right from the conceptualization to release. He has an in-depth understanding of business intelligence systems and hands-on experience with technologies such as Microsoft SQL Server, SQL Server Reporting Services, SQL Server Analysis Services, Web Services, ASP.NET, and Microsoft .NET. His achievements include innovative frameworks in reporting and analytics; he has been awarded five patents for his work in this area.

Manoj graduated with high honors from The University of Texas, Austin with a BS in Computer Science and an MS in Computer Science from The University of Washington, Seattle. He also holds an MBA in Finance from the Indian School of Business, Hyderabad.

Umesh Pandit is a Techno-functional Consultant with KPIT Cummins Infosystems Ltd. He has done a Master of Computer Applications with first division having specialized in ERP from the Ideal Institute of Technology, Ghaziabad.

Umesh has worked with top IT giants such as Google India and Capgemini India. He has a deep understanding of ERP systems such as Microsoft Dynamics AX. He has worked with different versions of Axapta like AX 3.0, AX 4.0, AX 5.0 (AX 2009), and AX 6.0 (AX 2012). He has a vast knowledge as regards to Microsoft Technologies like SQL, CRM, TFS, Office, Window Server 2008, Windows Server 2003, Office 365, Microsoft Dynamics NAV, SSRS, SSAS, VSS, and VCS.

I would like to thank my friend Pramila Kumari who encouraged me to follow this passion.

www.PacktPub.com

Support files, eBooks, discount offers and more

You might want to visit www.PacktPub.com for support files and downloads related to your book.

Did you know that Packt offers eBook versions of every book published, with PDF and ePub files available? You can upgrade to the eBook version at www.PacktPub.com and as a print book customer, you are entitled to a discount on the eBook copy. Get in touch with us at service@packtpub.com for more details.

At www.PacktPub.com, you can also read a collection of free technical articles, sign up for a range of free newsletters and receive exclusive discounts and offers on Packt books and eBooks.

http://PacktLib.PacktPub.com

Do you need instant solutions to your IT questions? PacktLib is Packt's online digital book library. Here, you can access, read and search across Packt's entire library of books.

Why Subscribe?

- Fully searchable across every book published by Packt
- Copy and paste, print and bookmark content
- On demand and accessible via web browser

Free Access for Packt account holders

If you have an account with Packt at www.PacktPub.com, you can use this to access PacktLib today and view nine entirely free books. Simply use your login credentials for immediate access.

Instant Updates on New Packt Books

Get notified! Find out when new books are published by following @PacktEnterprise on Twitter, or the *Packt Enterprise* Facebook page.

Table of Contents

Preface   **1**

Chapter 1: Developing a Simple SSRS Report in Visual Studio   **7**

  Reporting services modes   **8**

    The Native mode   8

    The SharePoint integrated mode   9

  Walkthrough – Create an Auto Design report with AX Query   **10**

    Scenario   10

    Prerequisites   11

    Creating an AOT Query   11

    Creating a Report Model project   14

    Creating an Auto Design SSRS report   14

    Saving the report to AOT and deploying it to the Report Server   18

      Deploying using Microsoft Dynamics AX 2012 Management Shell   19

    Running the report   20

  Walkthrough – Creating a drill-through report   **21**

    Scenario   21

    Prerequisites   21

    Creating a Report Model project   22

    Creating reports   22

      Creating a Vendor list report   22

      Creating a Purchase order list report   24

      Creating a Purchase order details report   25

    Providing a drill-through action under designs   30

      Adding a parameter – the Purchase order list report   30

      Adding a parameter – the Purchase order details report   31

    Drill-through action   32

      The Vendor list report   32

      The Purchase order list report   33

Saving the report to AOT and deploying it to the Report Server	34
Preview	34
Summary	**35**
Chapter 2: Developing Advanced Reports in Visual Studio	**37**
Common controls	**38**
Textbox	38
Line	38
Table	38
Matrix	39
Rectangle	39
List	39
Image	39
Subreport	39
Chart	39
Gauge	39
Walkthrough – Creating a Matrix report	**40**
Scenario	40
Prerequisites	40
Creating a Report Model project	40
Creating a Matrix report using Auto Design	41
Saving the report to AOT and deploying it to the Report Server	43
Running the report	44
Walkthrough – Creating a Chart report	**45**
Scenario	45
Prerequisites	45
Creating an AOT Query	45
Creating a Report Model project	48
Creating an Auto Design SSRS report	48
Saving the report to AOT and deploying it to the Report Server	51
Deploying using Microsoft Dynamics AX 2012 Management Shell	51
Running the report	52
Summary	**53**
Chapter 3: Developing a Report from an External Data Source	**55**
Walkthrough – Creating a report using an external data source	**56**
Scenario	56
Prerequisites	56
Preparing report data	56
Creating a report project	58
Creating an external report data source	59

Creating reports   59
Modifying report appearances   61
Report preview   62
Summary   **62**

**Chapter 4: Importing Reports from Visual Studio to AX
and Report Deployment**   **63**
Adding a report to Visual Studio Project   **65**
Adding a report project to the AOT   **66**
Report deployment   **66**
Microsoft Dynamics AX   66
Microsoft Visual Studio   66
Microsoft Dynamics AX 2012 Management Shell   66
Summary   **67**

Chapter 5: Using Controller and User Interface Builder Classes   **69**
The Model-View-Controller   **69**
Model   69
View   70
Controller   70
The Controller class   **70**
The UI Builder class   **72**
The SrsReportDataContractUIBuilder class   72
The SysOperationAutomaticUIBuilder class   73
Summary   **73**

Chapter 6: Developing Reports Using RDP and Report Contracts   **75**
The Report data provider class   **76**
The Report contract class   **76**
Walkthrough – Creating an Auto Design report using the RDP class   **77**
Scenario   77
Prerequisites   77
Creating a Report data provider class   77
Creating a Report Model project   78
Creating a Table report using Auto Design   79
Saving to AOT, deploying, and running the report   82
Walkthrough – Creating a Precision Design report   **82**
Scenario   82
Creating a Precision Design from Auto Design   82
Adding totals to the Amount field   82
Adding a page break for each customer   83

Saving to AOT, deploying, and running the report	83
Walkthrough: Creating a report with parameters	**84**
Scenario	84
Prerequisites	84
Creating a contract class	84
Modifying RDP to accept the Report Contracts	86
Refreshing the Report Dataset for new parameters	86
Saving to AOT, deploying, and running the report	87
Summary	**87**
Chapter 7: Customizing Existing Microsoft Dynamics AX Reports Using Visual Studio	**89**
Editing existing reports in Visual Studio	**90**
Finding the SSRS Report Model Project in AOT	90
Saving changes to AX	92
Deploying changes to the Report Server	92
Enabling a sort order for Sales order ID	**93**
Adding parameters to control the data displayed in the report	**94**
Summary	**95**
Appendix A: Common SSRS Expressions	**97**
String functions	**97**
Appendix B: Common Standard AX Classes and Methods	**103**
Common classes and their purpose	**103**
Common methods and their purposes	**105**
Appendix C: Reporting Best Practices	**107**
Best practices for AX 2012 report development	**107**
Report table	107
Do's	107
Don'ts	108
The RDP class	108
Do's	108
Don'ts	108
The Contract class	108
Do's	108
Don'ts	109
The Controller class	109
Do's	109
Don'ts	109
The UI Builder class	109
Do's	109
Don'ts	109

Report design   110
   Do's   110
   Don'ts   110
AOT queries   110
   Do's   110
   Don'ts   110

Index   **111**

Preface

Businesses these days are growing rapidly, and every entity works on data, which is presented in a specific format so that strong decisions can be taken, or a real-time picture of the business can be seen. Higher managements seek for high-end reports, where data is aggregated and presented in the form of charts where they can easily compare their net margins, sales, and other aspects whereas the core departments require reports where they can analyze data at a micro level. Also, while presenting data to each end user, a hierarchy of security levels should be applied so that only the authenticated data owners can see their reports.

This increases a big need for a good reporting tool, which has the capability to deliver all reports required for the business, ranging from high-end aggregated data to transactional data, all in real time.

The **Microsoft Dynamics AX 2012 Reporting** framework was designed for all such kind of requirements. Reporting inside AX 2012 has been pretty strong which allows analyzing any kind of data with a minimal number of clicks. It also provides a development framework which any developer/administrator can develop or manage various reports inside AX.

In this book, we will take a close look at all the features of Microsoft Dynamics AX 2012 Reporting, and we will develop various reports using step-by-step walkthroughs which will boost your confidence about reporting in AX 2012.

What this book covers

Chapter 1, *Developing a Simple SSRS Report in Visual Studio*, covers AX reporting basics, common SSRS terms, walkthroughs for developing simple SSRS reports, and the drill-through report.

Chapter 2, *Developing Advanced Reports in Visual Studio*, describes the common SSRS reporting tools, walkthroughs for creating a Matrix report and a Chart report.

Chapter 3, Developing a Report from an External Data Source, covers a walkthrough about how to build reports which connect to the external database inside AX.

Chapter 4, Importing Reports from Visual Studio to AX and Report Deployment, deals with various topics, such as how to add new/existing reports to the report project in Visual Studio and saving to AOT. It also explains about various methods of deploying reports to the Report Server.

Chapter 5, Using Controller and User Interface Builder Classes, provides knowledge about the Model-View-Controller pattern which is used for the AX reporting framework. It also explains about implementing the `Controller` and `UI Builder` classes to build reports.

Chapter 6, Developing Reports Using RDP and Report Contracts, covers **Report data provider** (**RDP**) and **Report contracts**. It explains how we can implement these classes for our reporting needs. You can easily learn the same by following the step-by-step walkthroughs provided.

Chapter 7, Customizing Existing Microsoft Dynamics AX Reports Using Visual Studio, explains how to customize existing reports using Visual Studio, you will get to learn about real-world problems of editing default reports.

Appendix A, Common SSRS Expressions, covers various SSRS expressions like `String`, `Date`, `Format`, and `Global` functions, which are often required at the time of the report development.

Appendix B, Common Standard AX Classes and Methods, covers various topics about all the Reporting classes and methods which are commonly used during report development.

Appendix C, Reporting Best Practices, deals with various best practices and design constraints, which should be kept in mind during report development. You will be able to learn about all the Do's and Don'ts for the `Reporting` table, the `RDP` class, the `Contract` class, the `Controller` class, the `UI Builder` class, report design, and AOT queries.

What you need for this book

All walkthroughs and exercises explained in this book were implemented on Microsoft Dynamics AX 2012 R2 Virtual Machine, which can be downloaded from the following link:

```
http://blogs.technet.com/b/dutchpts/archive/2012/12/23/microsoft-
dynamics-ax-2012-r2-demo-vm-available.aspx
```

The following is the list of software components which were used to implement walkthroughs explained in this book:

- Microsoft Dynamics AX 2012 (Kernel version: 6.2.158.0, Application version: 6.2.158.0)
- Microsoft Visual Studio 2010 (Version: 10.0.40219.1 SP1Rel)
- Microsoft .NET Framework (Version: 4.5.50709 SP1Rel)
- Microsoft Windows Server 2008 R2 Enterprise (Service Pack 1)
- Microsoft Internet Explorer 9

Who this book is for

This book is great for developers and administrators who deal with Microsoft Dynamics AX 2012 Reporting in day-to-day scenarios. It assumes that you don't have any exposure to Dynamics AX 2012 reporting and will teach you from basic to advance level using real-time scenarios. It also mentions a few administrative tasks, which will help you manage reports. Readers must know about the AX architecture, AOT, basic X++ skills, and basics of SSRS.

Conventions

In this book, you will find a number of styles of text that distinguish between different kinds of information. Here are some examples of these styles, and an explanation of their meaning.

Code words in text are shown as follows: Rename Sorting to **AccountNum** and **SortBy** to `Fields!AccountNum.Value` under properties.

A block of code is set as follows:

```
[DataMemberAttribute("FromDate")]
public FromDate parmFromDate(FromDate _fromDate = fromDate){
  fromDate = _fromDate;
  return fromDate;
}
```

When we wish to draw your attention to a particular part of a code block, the relevant lines or items are set in bold:

```
[SRSReportParameterAttribute(classstr(SrsContractSample))]
class SrsRDPSample extends SRSReportDataProviderBase{
  CustTransTotalSales custTransTotalSales;
}
```

Any command-line input or output is written as follows:

```
Publish-AXReport -ReportName SalesCustomerChart
```

1. **New terms** and **important words** are shown in bold. Words that you see on the screen, in menus or dialog boxes for example, appear in the text like this: Create an Output menu item by right clicking **AOT | Menu Items | Output | New menu item**.

2. Information appears like below:

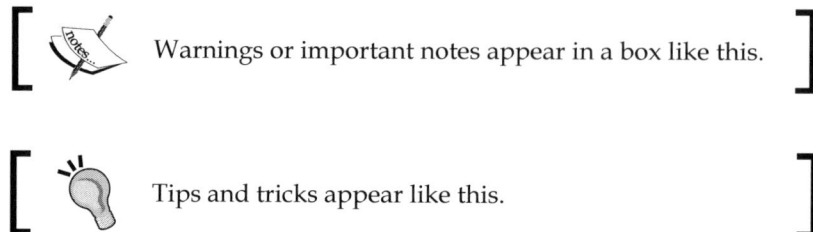

Warnings or important notes appear in a box like this.

Tips and tricks appear like this.

Reader feedback

Feedback from our readers is always welcome. Let us know what you think about this book—what you liked or may have disliked. Reader feedback is important for us to develop titles that you really get the most out of.

To send us general feedback, simply send an e-mail to feedback@packtpub.com, and mention the book title via the subject of your message.

If there is a topic that you have expertise in and you are interested in either writing or contributing to a book, see our author guide on www.packtpub.com/authors.

Customer support

Now that you are the proud owner of a Packt book, we have a number of things to help you to get the most from your purchase.

Downloading the example code

You can download the example code files for all Packt books you have purchased from your account at http://www.packtpub.com. If you purchased this book elsewhere, you can visit http://www.packtpub.com/support and register to have the files e-mailed directly to you.

Errata

Although we have taken every care to ensure the accuracy of our content, mistakes do happen. If you find a mistake in one of our books—maybe a mistake in the text or the code—we would be grateful if you would report this to us. By doing so, you can save other readers from frustration and help us improve subsequent versions of this book. If you find any errata, please report them by visiting http://www.packtpub.com/submit-errata, selecting your book, clicking on the **errata submission form** link, and entering the details of your errata. Once your errata are verified, your submission will be accepted and the errata will be uploaded on our website, or added to any list of existing errata, under the Errata section of that title. Any existing errata can be viewed by selecting your title from http://www.packtpub.com/support.

Piracy

Piracy of copyright material on the Internet is an ongoing problem across all media. At Packt, we take the protection of our copyright and licenses very seriously. If you come across any illegal copies of our works, in any form, on the Internet, please provide us with the location address or website name immediately so that we can pursue a remedy.

Please contact us at copyright@packtpub.com with a link to the suspected pirated material.

We appreciate your help in protecting our authors, and our ability to bring you valuable content.

Questions

You can contact us at questions@packtpub.com if you are having a problem with any aspect of the book, and we will do our best to address it.

1

Developing a Simple SSRS Report in Visual Studio

SQL Server Reporting Services (SSRS) provides a full set of tools to develop various kinds of reports, manage them, and deploy them to multiple environments. It also provides an independent user interface where users can see all the reports and run them, or administrators can control security permissions for other users.

In this chapter we will also cover the following topics in detail:

- Reporting services modes
- Creating an **Application Object Tree (AOT)** query
- Creating a Report Model project
- Creating an Auto Design report
- Creating a drill-through report
- How to enable a drill-down action in multiple reports
- Saving and deploying a report

Microsoft SQL Server reporting services are used now for Microsoft Dynamics AX 2012 reporting requirements. All reports available in AX 2012 are based out of SSRS, and use a rich variety of capabilities available in standard SSRS.

To start with, let's talk about a few major terms which would be used under chapters written in this book.

Downloading the example code

You can download the example code files for all Packt books you have purchased from your account at http://www.packtpub.com. If you purchased this book elsewhere, you can visit http://www.packtpub.com/supportand register to have the files e-mailed directly to you.

Reporting services modes

SSRS supports two modes for managing the report catalog: Native mode and SharePoint integrated mode.

AX 2012 only supports Native mode, while AX 2012 R2 supports Integrated and SharePoint integrated mode.

The Native mode

In Native mode, a Report Server is a standalone application which does not talk to any other application. All Microsoft Dynamics AX 2012 reports are deployed and hosted in the Report Server which could be managed using Report manager.

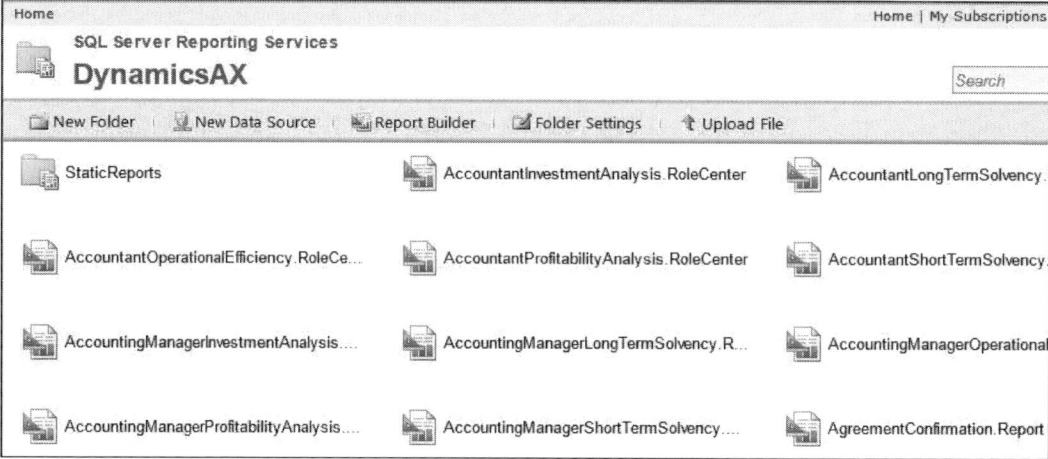

Screenshot 1: Report manager

SSRS Report Server can be opened in any web browser and looks like the following screenshot:

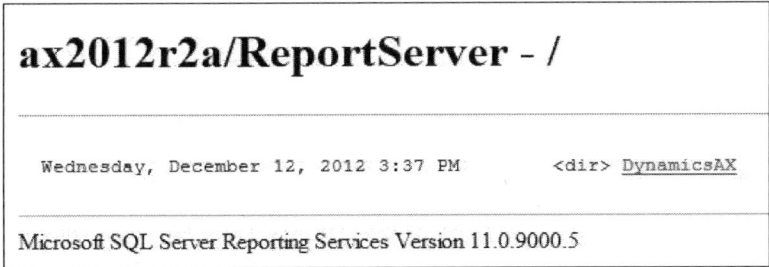

Screenshot 2: Report Server

The SharePoint integrated mode

In **SharePoint integrated mode,** a Report Server runs in a SharePoint website web farm. All reports are deployed and hosted to a Reports library under a SharePoint library.

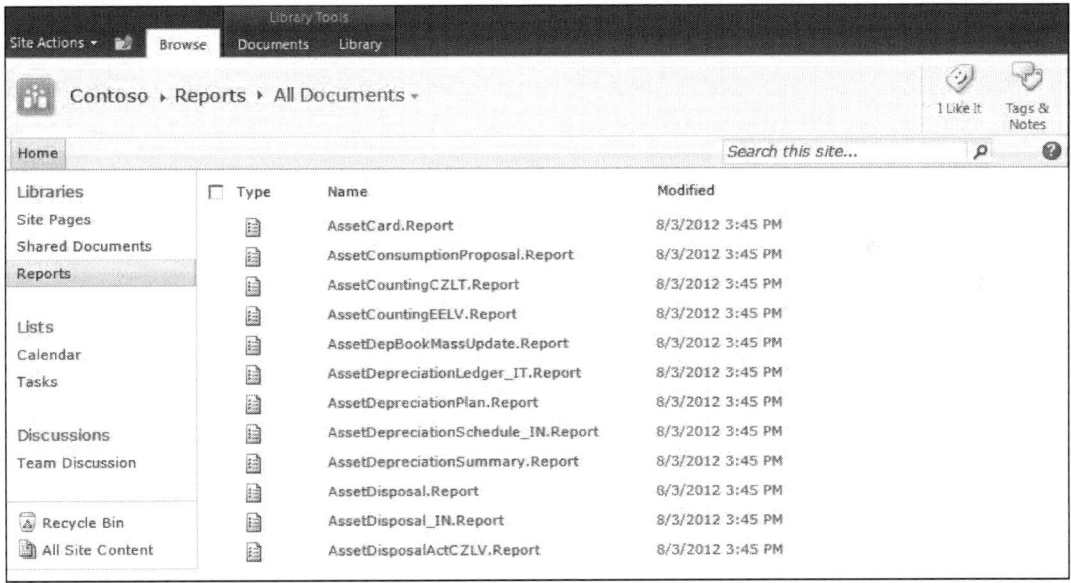

Screenshot 3: SharePoint integrated mode

Microsoft Dynamics AX 2012 has been tightly integrated with Visual Studio 2010, which enables administrators/developers to develop SSRS reports in Visual Studio Integrated Development Environment easily.

Visual Studio provides the ability to create various types of SSRS reports for Microsoft Dynamics AX 2012. Administrators/Developers can create a Report Model project in Visual Studio which hosts multiple SSRS reports.

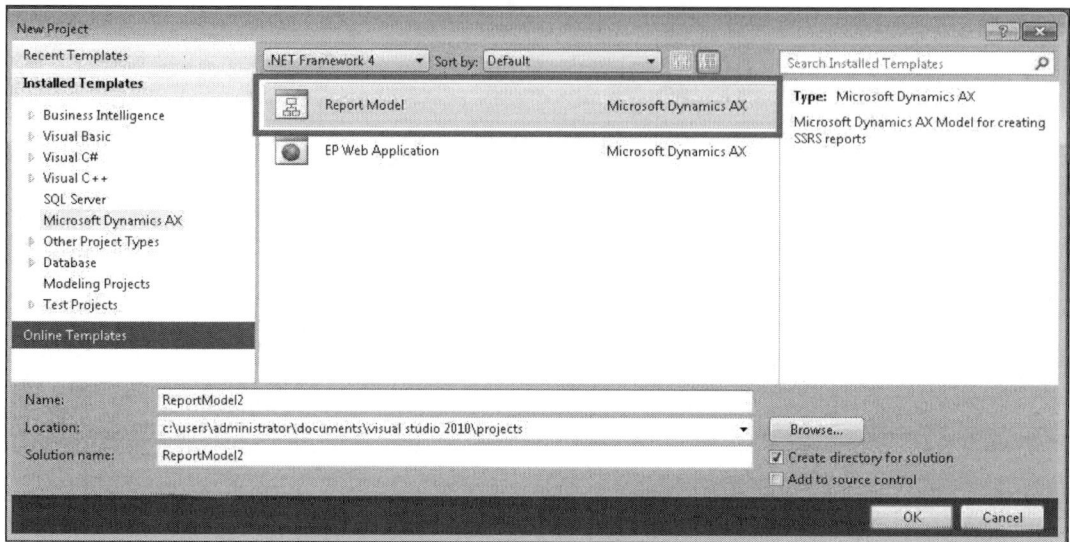

Screenshot 4: Visual Studio reporting capabilities

Walkthrough – Create an Auto Design report with AX Query

Scenario

Matt — A Customer relationship manager, wants to see all his customers and their respective transactions in a report to see how well the company is able to manage customers, and which customer is providing them better sales.

This walkthrough illustrates the following tasks:

- Creating an AOT Query
- Creating a Report Model project
- Creating an Auto Design SSRS Report
- Saving the report to AOT and deploying it to the Report Server

Prerequisites

To learn and implement the following walkthrough, you must have:

- Microsoft Dynamics AX 2012 with sample data
- Microsoft Visual Studio 2010 with Microsoft Dynamics AX reporting extension
- Microsoft Dynamics SQL Server Reporting Services

Creating an AOT Query

1. Open Microsoft Dynamics AX 2012 from the Start menu.
2. Open Development Workspace. There are multiple ways to do this which are described as follows:
    1. Press *Ctrl + D* to open AOT in Development Workspace.
    2. Press *Ctrl + Shift + P* to open **Projects** in Development Workspace.
    3. Press *Alt + W* to open windows and navigate to **New Development Workspace**.
    4. Press *Ctrl + Shift + W* to open **New Development Workspace**.
3. Go to **AOT | Queries** node.
4. Right-click on the **Queries** node and click on **New Query**.
5. Right-click on the newly created query and navigate to **Properties**.

6. Set the following properties:

    1. Provide **Name** as `CustTransReport`.

    2. Provide **Title** as `Customer transactions`.

    3. Provide **Descriptions** as **All Customer transactions**.

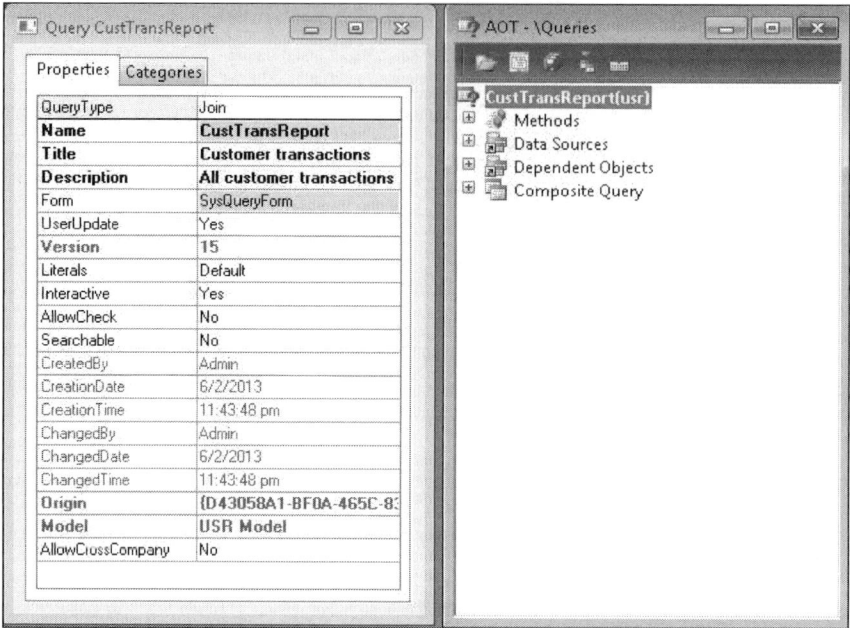

Screenshot 5: Query

7. Under **CusTransReport**, right-click on **Data Sources**, and select **New Data Source**.

8. Set the **Table** property for the new data source to **CustTable**.

9. Select the **Fields** node and set Dynamic Property to **Yes**.

10. Right-click on the **Data Sources** node and select new data source under **CustTable_1** data source.

11. Set the **Table** property for new data source to **CustTrans**, also set **Relations** property to **Yes**.

12. Select the **Fields** node and set the Dynamic property to **Yes** under **CustTrans_1** data source.

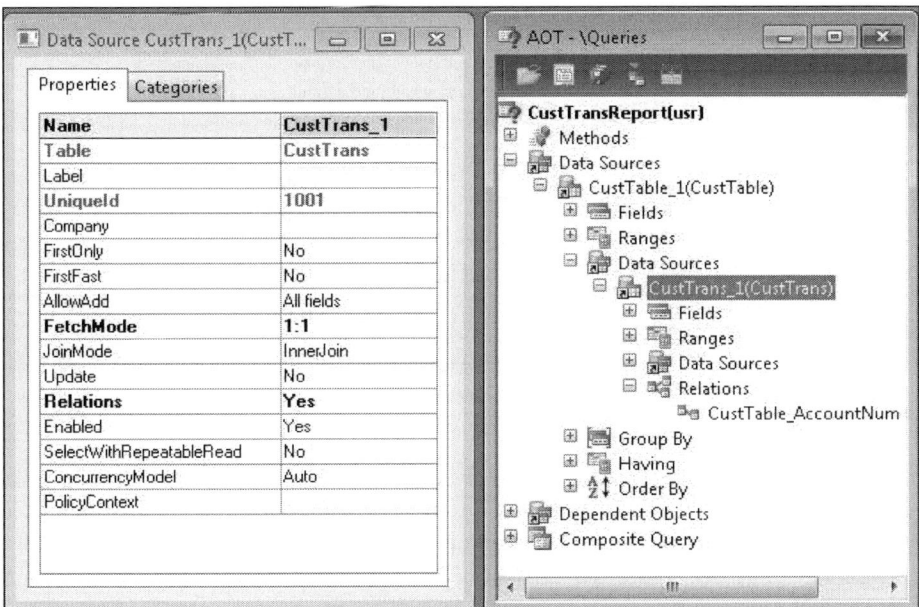

Screenshot 6: Data sources under query

Creating a Report Model project

1. Start Visual Studio; press *Ctrl + N* to create a new project.

2. Select Microsoft Dynamics AX under **Installed Templates** in the left pane, and select **Report Model**.

3. Provide a name for the project as `CustTransReport`.

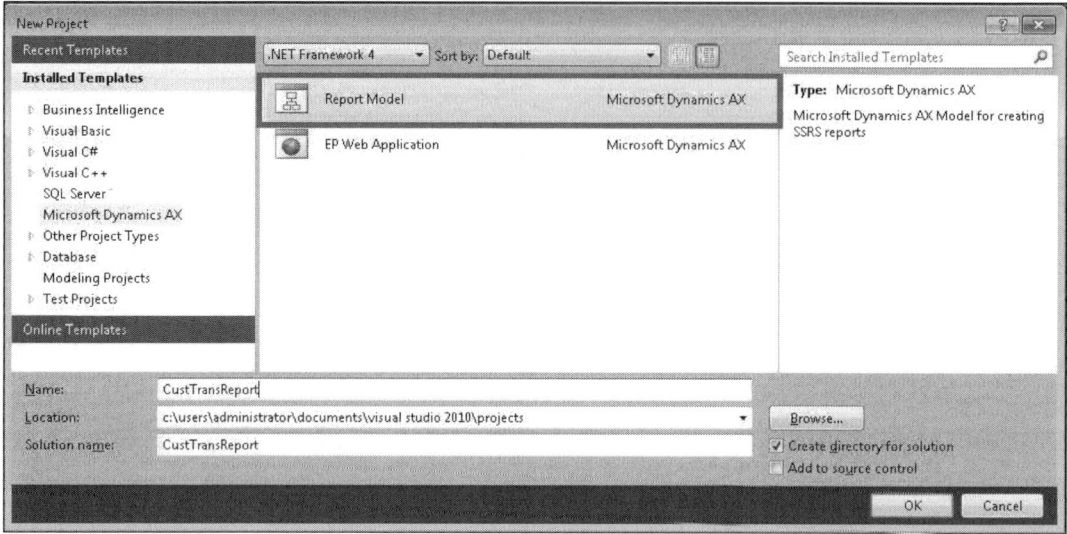

Screenshot 7: New visual studio project

Creating an Auto Design SSRS report

1. Right-click on **Solution**; navigate to **Report** under Add submenu. Select the report and rename it to `CustTransactions`.

2. Right-click on **Datasets** and click on **Add dataset**.

3. Modify the following properties for the newly added dataset:

    1. **Data Source** to **Microsoft Dynamics AX**.

    2. **Data Source Type** to **Query**.

    3. **Default Layout** to **Table**.

    4. **Name** to `CustTransDS`.

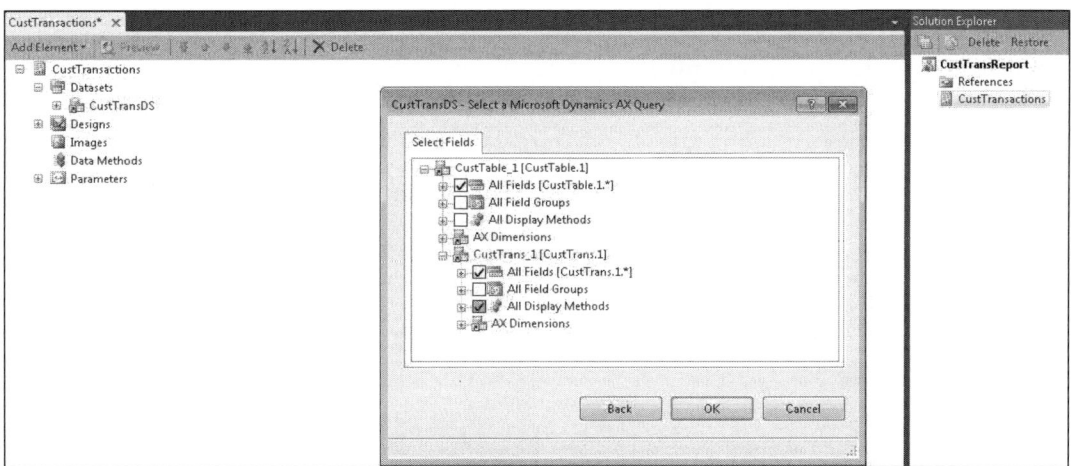

Screenshot 8: New dataset

4. Switch to the **Query** property, and press the button at the top right-hand corner to open the **Query** dialog.

5. Select **CustTransReport** from the list and press the **Next** button.

6. Select the **AccountNum, Name** fields from **CustTable_1**, and select **Voucher, TransType, TransDate, Invoice, AmountCur, remainAmountCur()** display methods, and **Currency** fields from **CustTrans_1** (Refer to Screenshot 4: New Dataset).

7. Drag-and-drop **CustTransDS** to the Design section of the report. This will create a new Auto Design named as **AutoDesign1**.

8. Select **AutoDesign1**, go to **Properties**, and set the following properties:

    1. **LayoutTemplate** to **ReportLayoutStyleTemplate**.

    2. **Title** to Customer transactions.

9. Select **CustTransDSTable** under **AutoDesign1** and set the following properties:

    1. **StyleTemplate** to **TableStyleAlternatingRowsTemplate**.

    2. **Title** to List of customer transactions.

10. Right-click on **Groupings** inside **CustTransDSTable** and select **Add Grouping**.

11. Rename the new grouping to `CustomerAcc`.

12. Right-click on **Group on** under **CustomerAcc** grouping and select **Add Group on**.

13. Rename the grouping to `AccountNum` and set Expression to `Fields!AccountNum.Value` in properties.

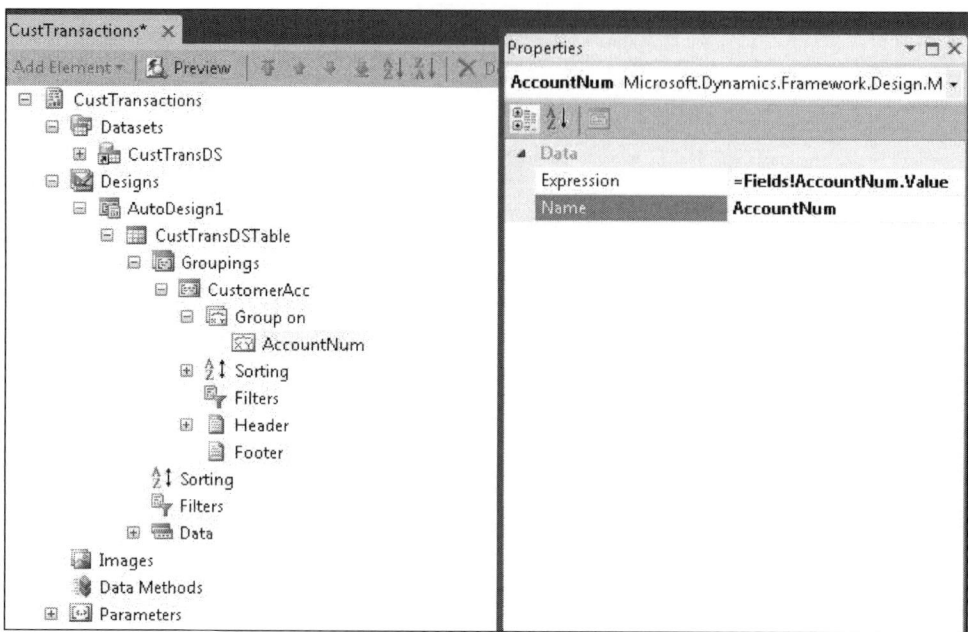

Screenshot 9: Grouping

14. Right-click on **Sorting** under **CustomerAcc** grouping and select **Add Sort**.

15. Rename **Sorting** to `AccountNum` and **SortBy** to `Fields!AccountNum.Value` under properties.

16. Right-click on **Header** under **CustomerAcc** grouping and select **Add row**.

17. Rename the row to `CustTableRow`.

18. Right-click on **CustTableRow** and select **Add | Field**.

19. Rename the field to `AccountNum` and set Expression to `Fields!AccountNum.Value`.

20. Right-click on **CustTableRow** and select **Add | Field**.

21. Rename the field to `Name` and set Expression to `Fields!Name.Value`.

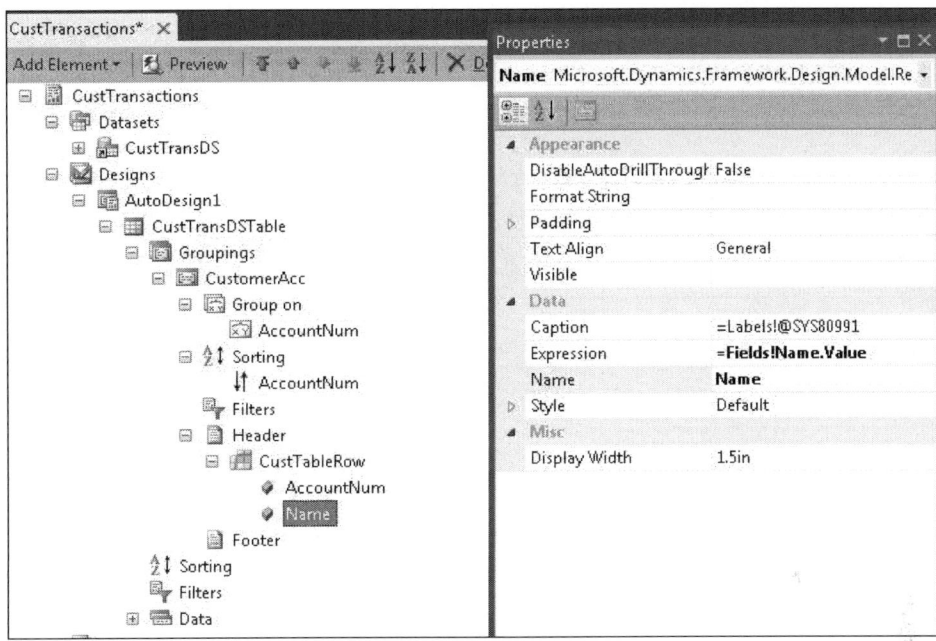

Screenshot 10: Header row

22. Go to the **Data** node under **CustTransDSTable** and verify that the following fields (Refer to the following screenshot) were correctly added automatically.

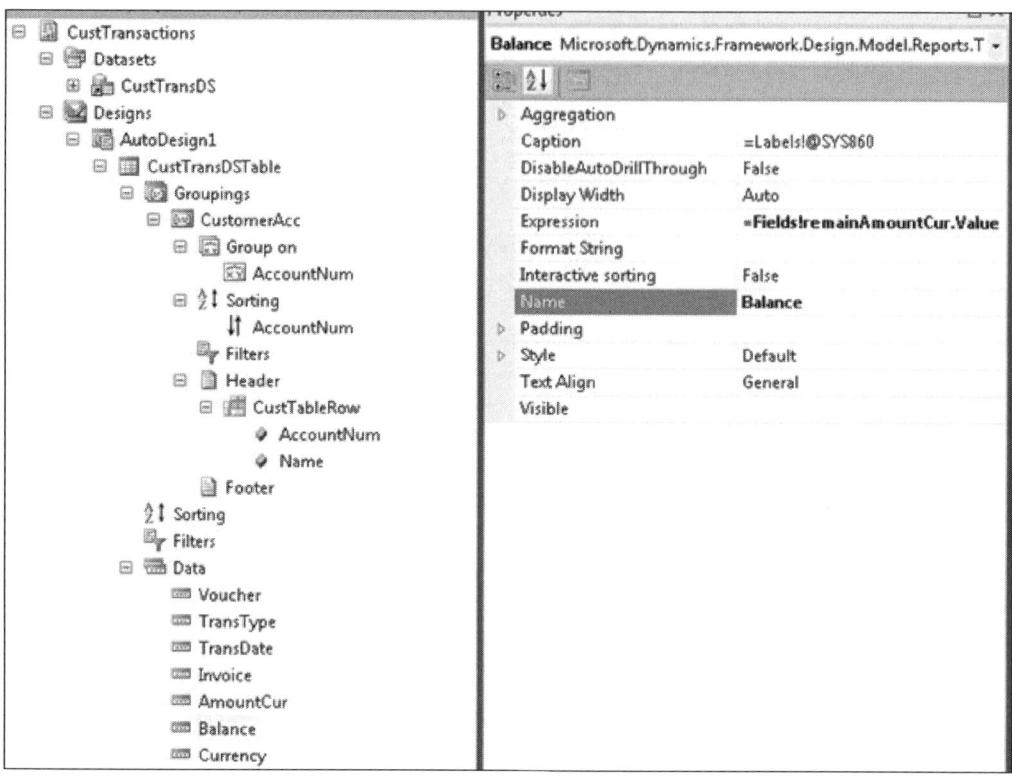

Screenshot 11: Adding fields to data

23. Save all changes done.

Saving the report to AOT and deploying it to the Report Server

1. In the Solution Explorer, right-click on the **Report Model** project and select **Build**.

2. Once the report is successfully built, right-click on the **Report Model** project and select **Add CustTransReport** to AOT.

3. We can deploy the report to the **Report Server**, once it has been added to **AOT**.

4. To deploy the report to the **Report Server**:

    1. Right-click on the **Report Model** project and select **Deploy**.
    2. Switch to AOT, right-click on **CustTransactions** report under **AOT | SSRS Reports | Deploy Element**.
    3. Deploy using **Microsoft Dynamics AX 2012 Management Shell**.

Deploying using Microsoft Dynamics AX 2012 Management Shell

The deployment can be done using the following steps:

1. Click on **Start | Administrative tools**.
2. Right-click on **Microsoft Dynamics AX 2012 Management Shell**.
3. Click on **Run as administrator**.
4. Enter the following PowerShell command to deploy.

```
Publish-AXReport -ReportName CustTransactions
```

```
Administrator: Microsoft Dynamics AX 2012 Management Shell
Importing AxUtilLib
Importing AxUtilLib.PowerShell
Importing Microsoft.Dynamics.Administration
Importing Microsoft.Dynamics.AX.Framework.Management
PS C:\Windows\system32> Publish-AXReport -ReportName "CustTransactions"
Deploying reports and related artifacts.


AOSName                     : 01@AX2012R2A
ConfigurationId             : WPPSJDCV221AXDBINTRS02
Description                 :
Default                     : True
ReportServerFolder          : DynamicsAX
ReportServerName            : AX2012R2A
ReportServerInstanceName    : AX2012R2A
ReportServerManagerUrl      : http://ax2012r2a/ReportServer
ReportServerWebServiceUrl   : http://ax2012r2a/ReportServer
SharePointIntegrated        : False

ReportName                  : CustTransactions
Designs                     : {CustTransactions.AutoDesign1}
Assemblies                  :
Datasources                 :
DesignDeploymentStatus      : {Success}
AssemblyDeploymentStatus    :
DataSourceDeploymentStatus  :

Deployment completed.

PS C:\Windows\system32> _
```

Screenshot 12: Deployment using Microsoft Dynamics AX 2012 Management Shell

Running the report

1. Create an Output menu item by right-clicking on **AOT | Menu Items | Output | New** menu item.

2. Rename the menu item to `CustTransactionsReport`.

3. Set the following properties:

    1. **Label** to `Customer transactions`.
    2. **HelpText** to `List of customer transactions`.
    3. **ObjectType** to **SSRSReport**.
    4. **Object** to **CustTransactions**.
    5. **ReportDesign** to **AutoDesign1**.

4. Save all changes.

5. Right-click on the **CustTransactionsReport** menu item and select **Open**.

6. Provide some dynamics filters if required.

7. Click **Ok** to run the report.

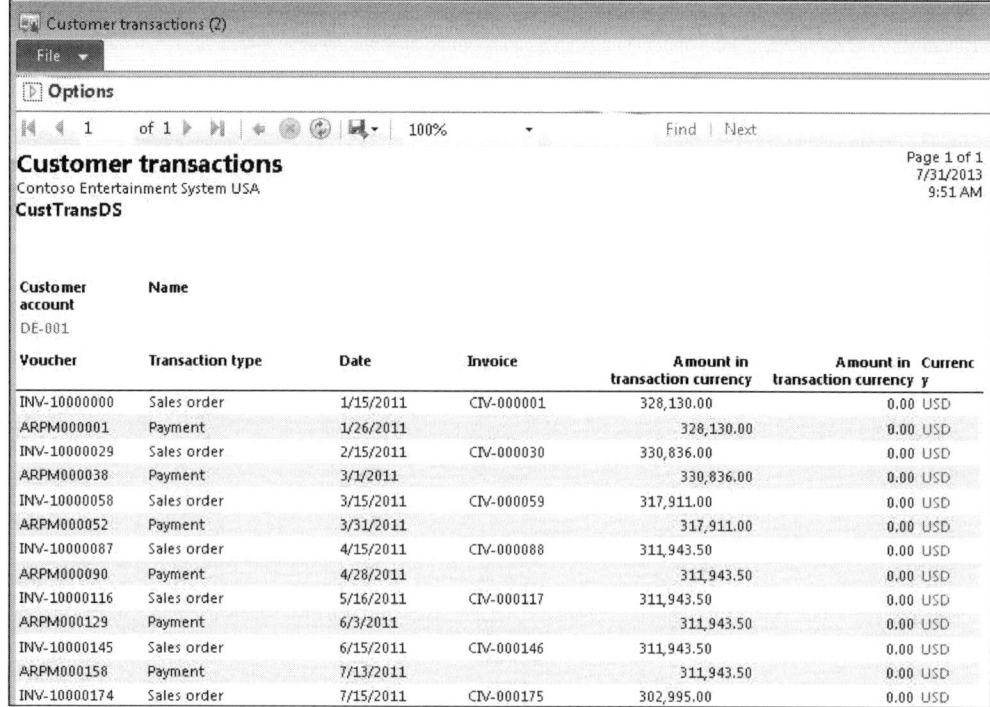

Screenshot 13: Final report

Walkthrough – Creating a drill-through report

Scenario

Tom— A Purchasing manager, wants to see all his vendors in a list and wants to iterate vendors to all of their purchase orders, and to their purchase order details. For this, he needs a report in the system which could display a list of vendors with drill-through capability to iterate to all purchase orders for the selected vendor, and also to the purchase order details when the purchase order ID is selected.

This walkthrough illustrates the following tasks:

- Creating a Report Model project.
- Creating reports
    - Vendor list
    - Purchase order list
    - Purchase order details
- Providing drill-through action under designs
- Saving the report to AOT and deploying it to the Report Server.

Prerequisites

To learn and implement the following walkthrough, you must have:

- Microsoft Dynamics AX 2012 with sample data.
- Microsoft Visual Studio 2010 with Microsoft Dynamics AX reporting extension.
- Microsoft Dynamics SQL Server Reporting Services.

Creating a Report Model project

1. Start Visual Studio; press *Ctrl + N* to create a new project.

2. Select Microsoft Dynamics AX under **Installed Templates** in the left pane, and select **Report Model**.

3. Provide a name for the project as VendPurchaseOrders.

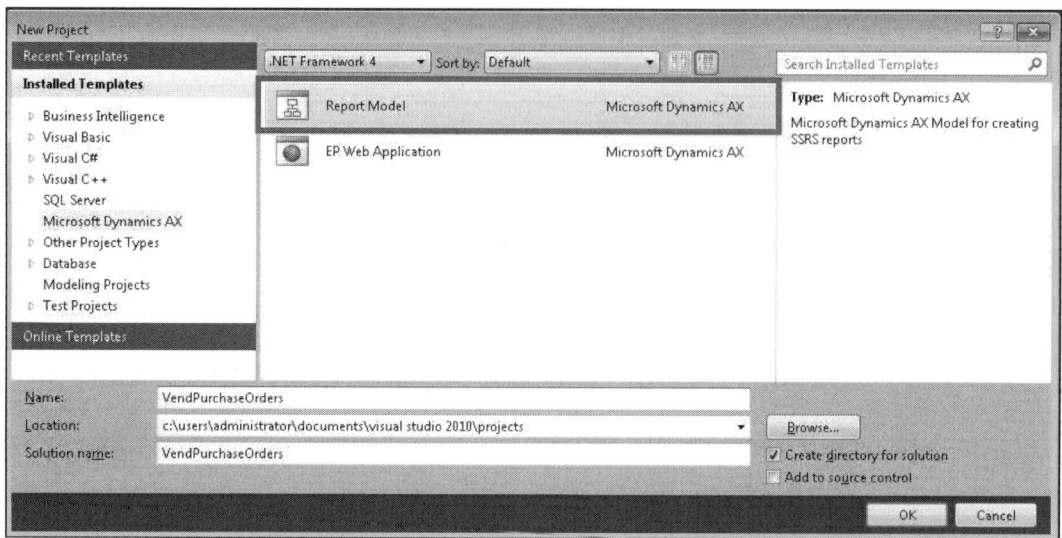

Screenshot 14: New visual studio project

Creating reports

Creating a Vendor list report

1. Right-click on **Solution** and navigate to **Report** under the **Add** submenu. Select the report and rename it to VendListRep.

2. Right-click on datasets and click on **Add dataset**.

3. Modify the following properties for the newly added dataset:

    1. **Data source** to **Microsoft Dynamics AX**.

    2. **Data source type** to **Query**.

    3. **Default Layout** to **Table**.

    4. **Name** to VendListDS.

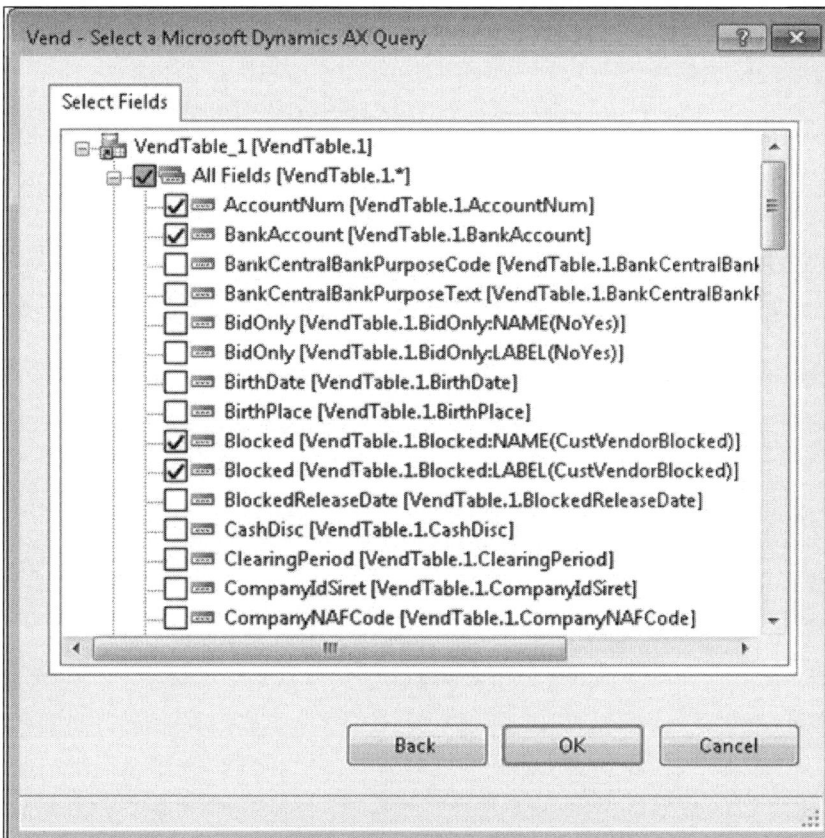

Screenshot 15: New dataset

4. Switch to the **Query** property and click on the blue button with white dots to open the **Query** dialog.

5. Select **VendBaseDataView** from the list and press the **Next** button.

6. Select **AccountNum, vendName** display methods; **BankAccount, Blocked, Invoice** fields from **VendTable_1** (Refer to Screenshot 2: New Dataset).

7. Drag-and-drop **VendListDS** to the Design section of the report. This will create a new Auto Design named as **AutoDesign1**.

8. Select **AutoDesign1**, go to **Properties**, and set the following properties:

    1. **LayoutTemplate** to **ReportLayoutStyleTemplate**.

    2. **Title** to Vendors.

9. Select **VendListDSTable** under **AutoDesign1** and set the following properties:

    1. **StyleTemplate** to **TableStyleAlternatingRowsTemplate**.
    2. **Title** to List of vendors.

Creating a Purchase order list report

1. Right-click on **Solution**; select **Report** under the **Add** submenu. Select the report and rename it to VendPurchOrders.
2. Right-click on datasets and click on **Add dataset**.
3. Modify the following properties for the newly added dataset

    1. **Data source** to **Microsoft Dynamics AX**.
    2. **Data source type** to **Query**.
    3. **Default Layout** to **Table**.
    4. **Name** to PurchOrderListDS.

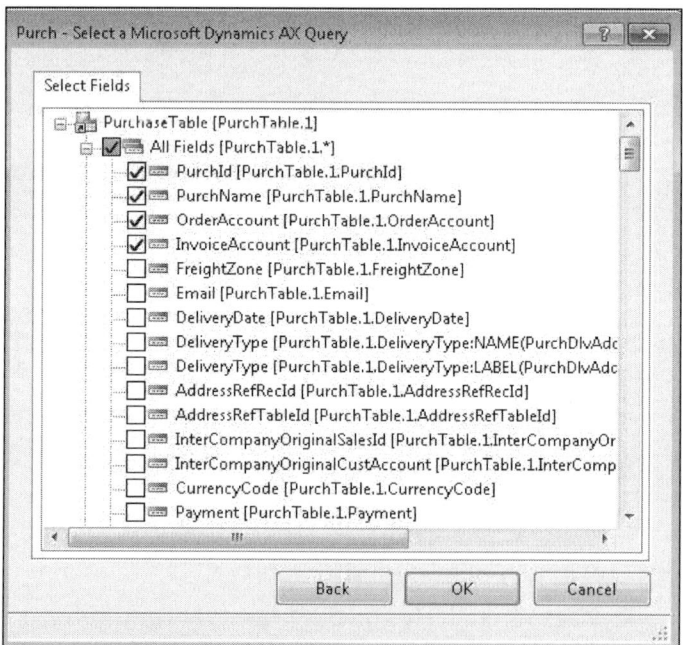

Screenshot 16: New dataset

4. Switch to the **Query** property and press the ⬚ icon to open the **Query** dialog.

5. Select **PurchTableListPage** from the list and press the **Next** button.

6. Select **PurchId, PurchName, OrderAccount, InvoiceAccount, PurchStatus, PurchaseType** fields from **PurchaseTable** (Refer to Screenshot 3: New Dataset).

7. Drag-and-drop **PurchOrderListDS** to the Design section of the report. This will create a new Auto Design named as **AutoDesign1**.

8. Select **AutoDesign1**, go to **Properties**, and set the following properties:

    1. **LayoutTemplate** as **ReportLayoutStyleTemplate**.

    2. **Title** as `Purchase orders`.

9. Select **PurchOrderListDSTable** under AutoDesign1 and set the following properties:

    1. **StyleTemplate** as **TableStyleAlternatingRowsTemplate**.

    2. **Title** as `List of purchase orders`.

Creating a Purchase order details report

1. Right-click on Solution, select Report under Add submenu. Select report, rename the report to `PurchDetails`.

2. Right-click on datasets, click on **Add dataset**.

3. Modify the following properties for the newly added dataset:

    1. **Data source** to **Microsoft Dynamics AX**.

    2. **Data source type** to **Query**.

    3. **Default Layout** to **Table**.

4.   **Name** to PurchDetailDS.

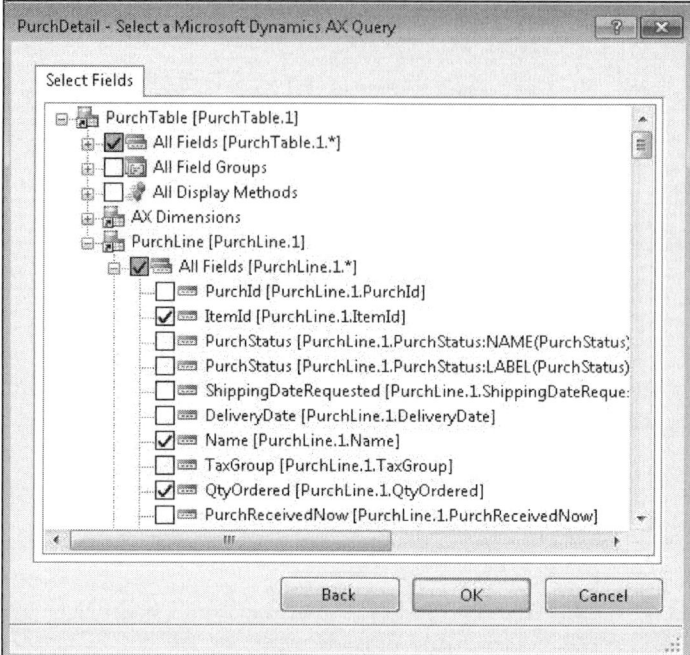

Screenshot 17: New dataset

4.   Switch to the **Query** property, and click on the button at the corner to open the **Query** dialog.

5.   Select **PurchTableDocument** from the list and click on the **Next** button.

6.   Select **PurchId**, **PurchName**, **OrderAccount**, **InvoiceAccount**, **Email**, **DeliveryDate** fields from **PurchTable**, and select **ItemId**, **Name**, **QtyOrdered**, **PriceUnit**, **PurchPrice**, and **CurrencyCode**, **LineAmount** fields from **PurchLine** (Refer to Screenshot 4: New Dataset).

7.   Drag-and-drop **PurchDetailDS** to the Design section of the report. This will create a new Auto Design named as **AutoDesign1**.

8.   Select **AutoDesign1**, go to **Properties**, and set the following properties:

1.   **LayoutTemplate** to **ReportLayoutStyleTemplate**.

2.   **Title** to Purchase order details.

9. Select **PurchDetailDSTable** under **AutoDesign1**, and set the following properties:

    1. **StyleTemplate** to **TableStyleAlternatingRowsTemplate**.

    2. **Title** to `Purchase order details`.

10. Right-click on **Groupings** inside **PurchDetailDSTable**, and select **Add Grouping**.

11. Rename the new grouping to `PurchId`.

12. Right-click on **Group On** under **PurchId** grouping and select **Add Group on**.

13. Rename **Grouping** to `PurchIdGrp` and set **Expression** to `Fields!PurchId.Value` in **Properties**.

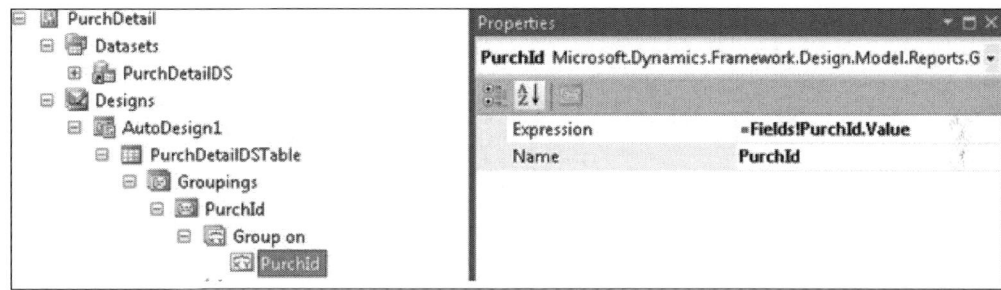

Screenshot 18: Adding a PurchId group

14. Right-click on **Header** under **PurchId** grouping, and select **Add row**.

15. Rename the row to `PurchTableRow`.

16. Right-click on **PurchTableRow** and select **Add | Field**.

17. Rename the field to `PurchId` and set **Expression** to `Fields!PurchId.Value`.

18. Right-click on **PurchTableRow** and navigate to **Add | Field**.

19. Rename the field to `Name` and set **Expression** to `Fields!PurchName.Value`.

20. Right-click on **PurchTableRow** and select **Add | Field**.

21. Rename the field to `Name` and set **Expression** to `Fields!OrderAccount.Value`.

22. Right-click on **PurchTableRow** and select **Add | Field**.

23. Rename the field to `Name` and set **Expression** to `Fields!InvoiceAccount.Value`.

24. Right-click on **PurchTableRow** and select **Add | Field**.

25. Rename the field to Name and set **Expression** to Fields!Email.Value.

26. Right-click on **PurchTableRow** and select **Add | Field**.

27. Rename the field to Name and set **Expression** to Fields!DeliveryDate.Value

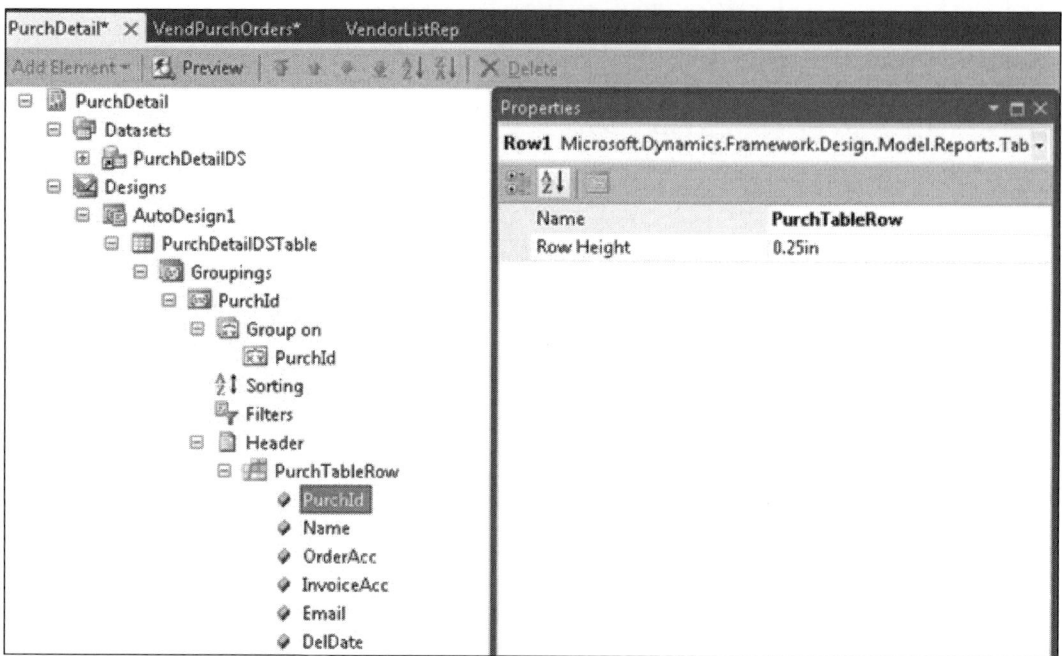

Screenshot 19: Header row

28. Go to the **Data** node under **PurchDetailDSTable** and verify that the following fields were correctly added automatically.

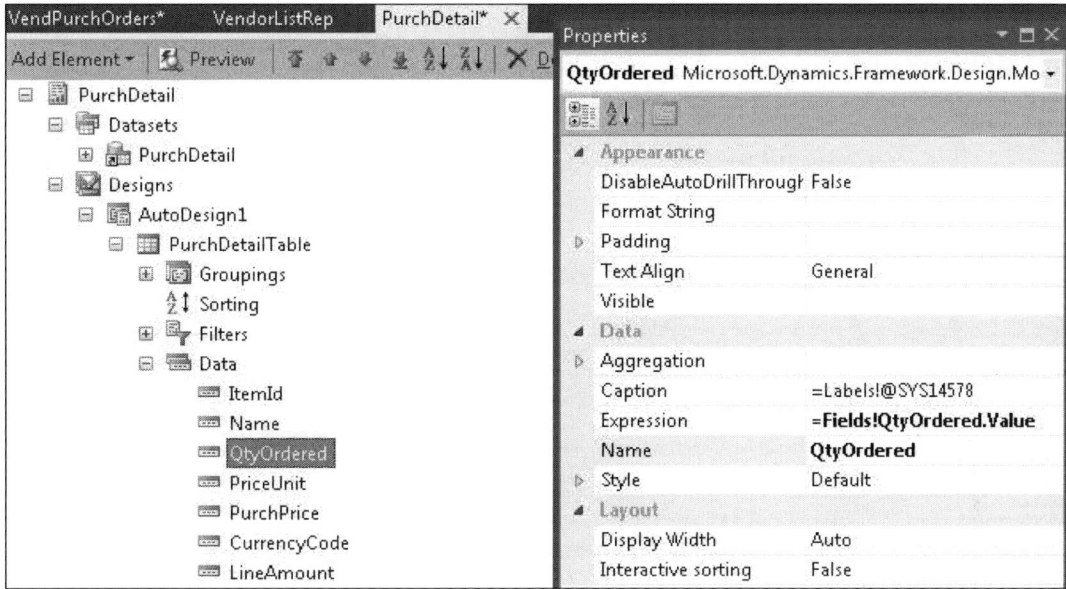

Screenshot 20: Adding fields to the data section

29. Save all changes done.

Providing a drill-through action under designs

Adding a parameter – the Purchase order list report

1. Right-click on **Parameters** and select **Add | Parameter**.

2. Rename the parameter to VendAccount.

3. Right-click on **filters**, and select **Add Filter** under **VendPurchOrders** report.

4. Rename the filter to VendAccount and set the following properties:

    1. **Expression** to Fields!OrderAccount.Value.

    2. **Name** to VendAccount.

    3. **Operator** to **Equals**.

    4. **Value** to Parameters!VendAccount.Value.

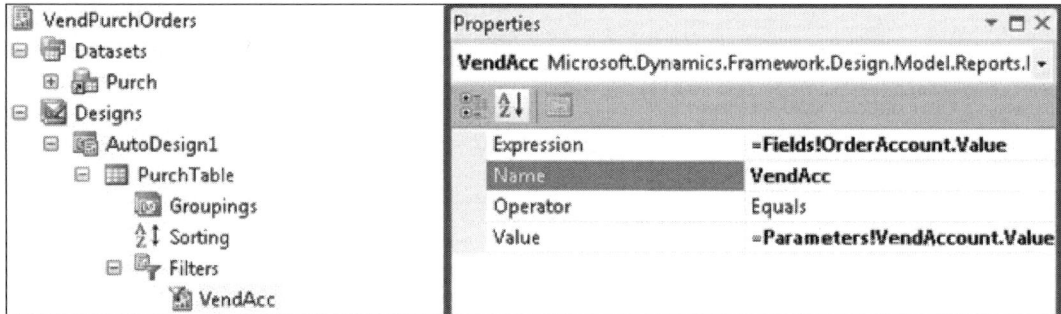

Screenshot 21: Adding a filter to a Purchase order list report

Adding a parameter – the Purchase order details report

1. Right-click on **Parameters**, and select **Add | Parameter**.

2. Rename the parameter to `PurchId`.

3. Right-click on **filters**, and select **Add Filter** under **PurchDetails** report.

4. Rename the filter to `PurchId` and set the following properties:

    1. **Expression** as `Fields!PurchId.Value`.

    2. **Name** as `PurchId`.

    3. **Operator** as **Equals**.

    4. **Value** as `Parameters!PurchId.Value`.

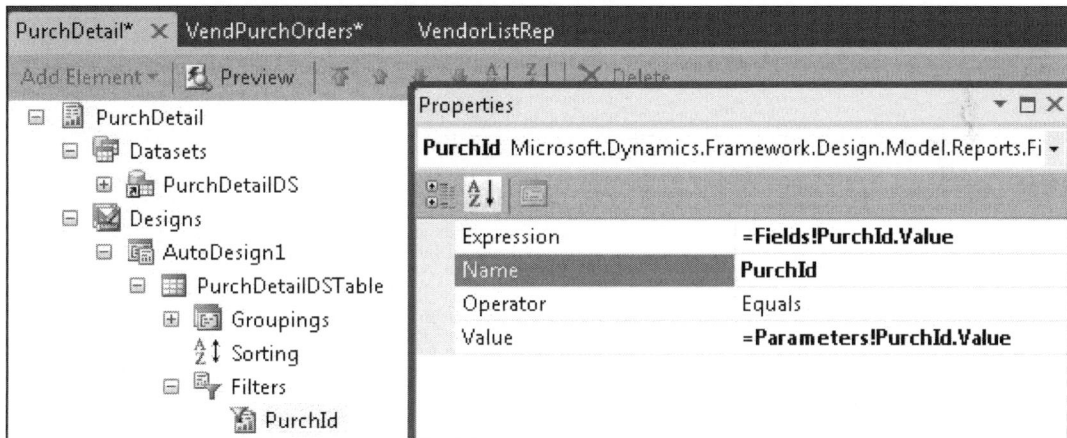

Screenshot 22: Adding a filter to a Purchase order details report

Drill-through action

The Vendor list report

1. Right-click on **AccountNum,** and select **Add Report Drill Through Action** under **AutoDesign1 | VendListDSTable | Data.**

2. Select **ReportDrillThroughAction** and go to **Properties.**

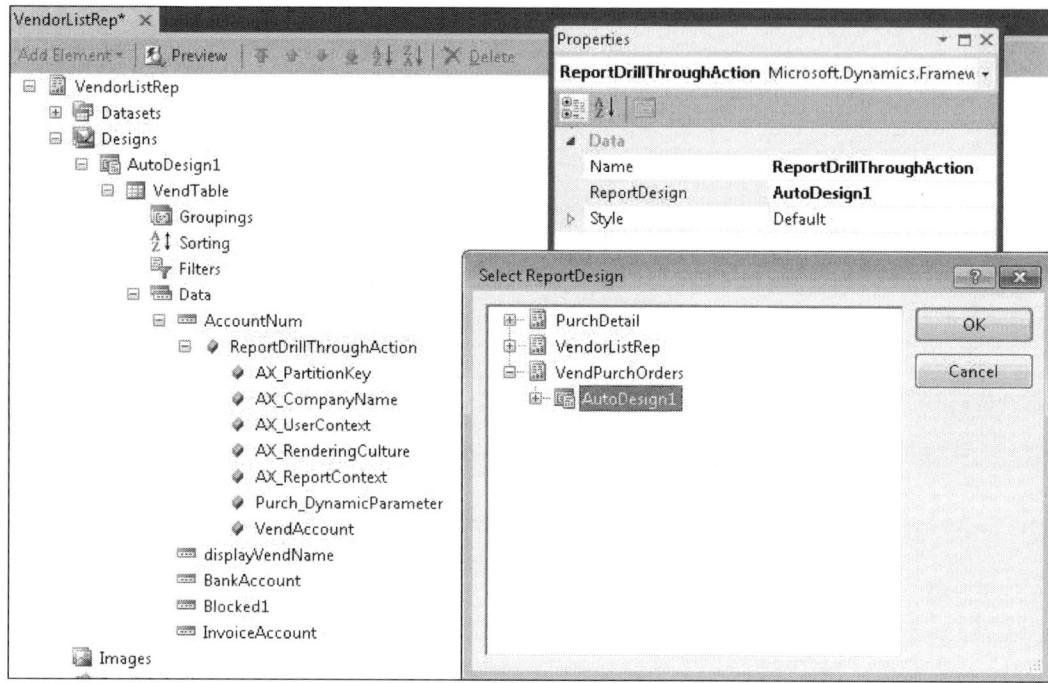

Screenshot 23: ReportDrillThroughAction for Vendor list report

3. Set the **ReportDesign** property to **AutoDesign1** of **VendPurchOrders** report.

4. Select the **AX_CompanyName** parameter under **ReportDrillThroughAction** and set the value to `Parameters!AX_CompanyName.Value`.

5. Select the **VendAccount** parameter under **ReportDrillThroughAction** and set value to `Fields!AccountNum.Value`.

The Purchase order list report

1. Right-click on **PurchId**, and select **Add Report Drill Through Action** under **AutoDesign1 | PurchOrderListDSTable | Data**.

2. Select **ReportDrillThroughAction** and go to **Properties**.

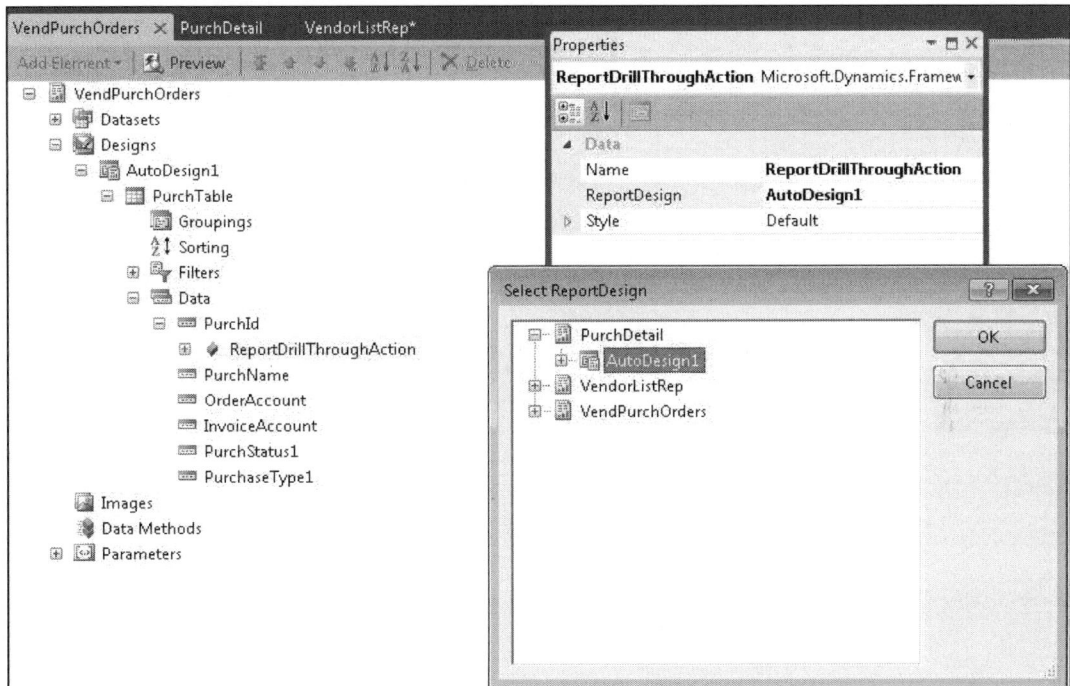

Screenshot 24: ReportDrillThroughAction to Purchase order details report

3. Set the **ReportDesign** property to **AutoDesign1** of **PurchDetails** report.

4. Select the **AX_CompanyName** parameter under **ReportDrillThroughAction** and set the value to `Parameters!AX_CompanyName.Value`.

5. Select the **PurchId** parameter under **ReportDrillThroughAction** and set the value to `Fields!PurchId.Value`.

Saving the report to AOT and deploying it to the Report Server

1. In the Solution Explorer, right-click on the **Report Model** project, and select Build.

2. Once the report is successfully built, right-click on the **Report Model** project, and select **Add VendPurchaseOrders to AOT**.

3. Once the report is added to AOT, we can deploy the same to the **Report Server**.

4. To deploy the report to the Report Server:

    1. Right-click on the **Report Model** project and select **Deploy**.

Preview

The Vendor list will be as follows:

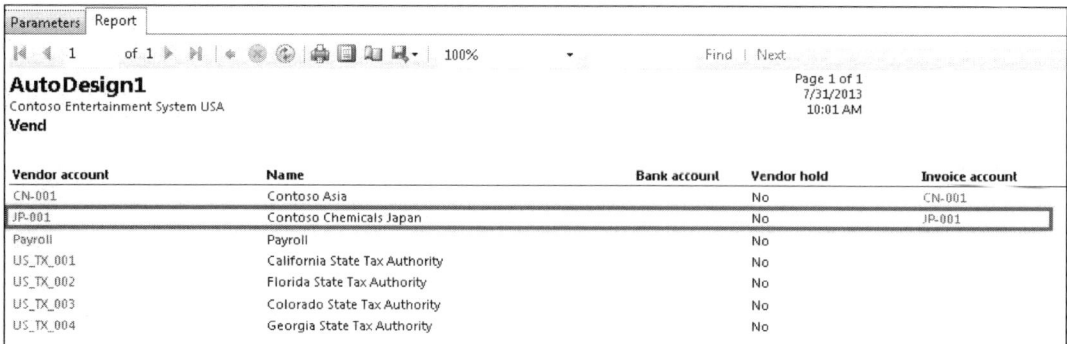

Screenshot 25: All purchase orders for the selected vendor

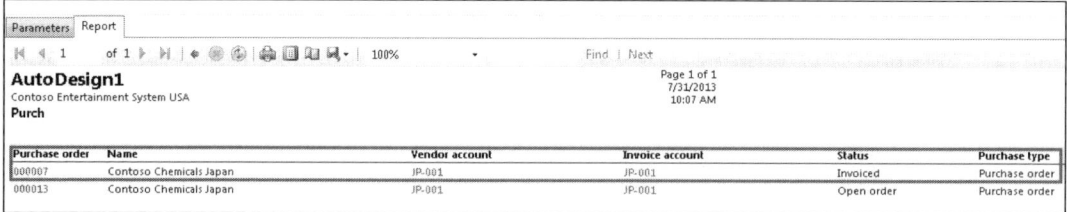

Screenshot 26: Purchase order details for the selected Purchase order

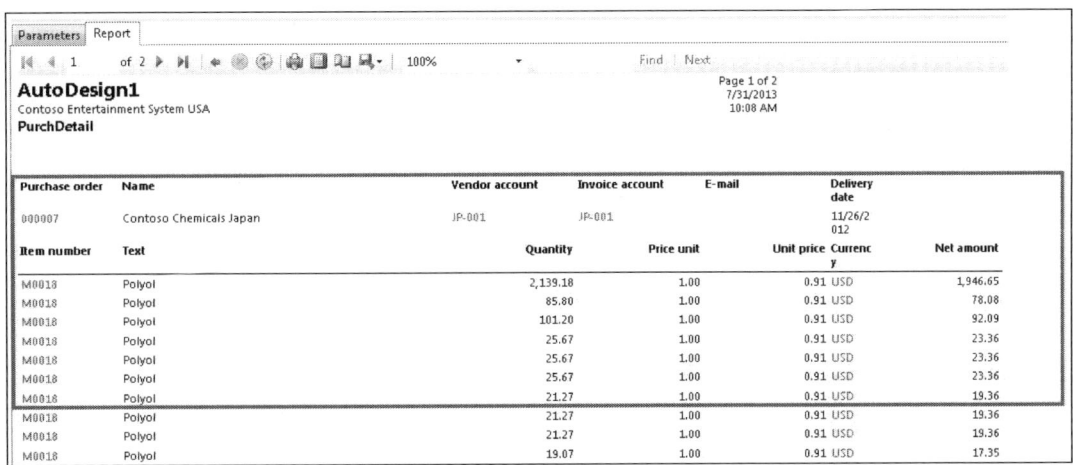

Screenshot 27: Final report

Summary

In this chapter we discussed the various reporting services modes and how to create a variety of reports for Microsoft Dynamics AX 2012 using Visual Studio. It is recommended to draw a design to analyze how, and what, report has to show, and then perform the development work, as it will give a clear picture about the development work to be done, and the correct way of developing a report can be chosen wisely.

In the next chapter we will learn how to develop advanced reports for Microsoft Dynamics AX 2012 using Visual Studio.

2
Developing Advanced Reports in Visual Studio

In this chapter, we will talk about creating advanced reports in Visual Studio and we will cover the following topics in detail:

- Common report controls
- Creating a Report Model project
- Creating a Matrix report
- Creating a Chart report
- Saving and deploying a report

Microsoft Dynamics AX 2012 is tightly integrated with Visual Studio, which provides a rich set of tools for advanced reporting. Visual Studio IDE provides almost the same interface as **SQL Business Intelligence Studio**, which allows report developers and administrators to develop/modify AX 2012 reports easily.

Developers can use various tools while designing reports from **Toolbox**. It can be opened from the **View** menu in Visual Studio, or by using the shortcut *Ctrl + W, X*.

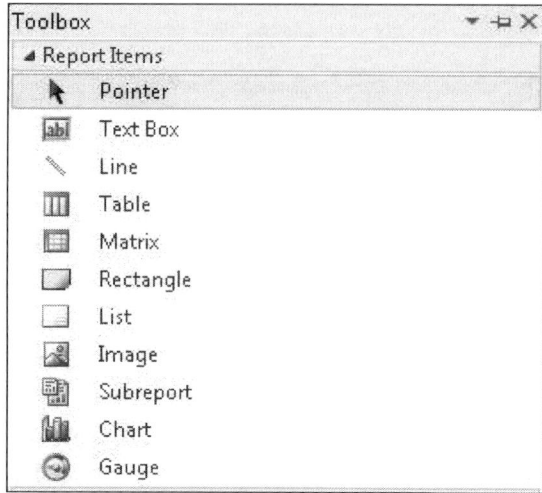

Screenshot 1: Toolbox

Common controls

Some of the common controls are as follows:

Textbox

The **Text Box** control allows displaying custom text or a dataset field value.

The value for the text box can be written in its expression. For example, if you need to display today's date, then the expression could be [="Today's date is " + today()].

Line

The **Line** control allows adding a line in the report design.

Table

The **Table** control allows displaying multiple records, where rows are dynamic and columns are static.

Matrix

The **Matrix** control allows displaying multiple records, where rows and columns are dynamic.

Rectangle

The **Rectangle** control allows displaying a rectangle shape in the report design.

List

The **List** control allows displaying a list of data in the report design.

Image

The **Image** control allows displaying an image in the report design. The image could be loaded from the filesystem or from a database.

Subreport

The **Subreport** control allows the user to add a report within a report. It gives more flexibility to users to perform analysis, such as sales by region. A report displays transactions region wise, and when a user selects a region, a chart gets loaded which shows sales by region and period wise.

Chart

The **Chart** control allows displaying data in the form of a chart, and it gives an easy understandability to the users while analyzing data. We can develop Column charts, Bar charts, Line charts, Pie charts, and Doughnut charts using AX 2012.

Gauge

The **Gauge** control allows displaying data in the form of a Gauge. It could be of any type, radial or linear.

Walkthrough – Creating a Matrix report

Scenario

John, a Sales manager, needs a report in which he could easily understand which customers have given top sales to the business year wise.

This walkthrough illustrates the following tasks:

- Creating a Report Model project
- Creating a Matrix report using Auto Design
- Saving the report to AOT and deploying it to the Report Server
- Running the report

Prerequisites

To learn and implement the following walkthrough, you must have:

- Microsoft Dynamics AX 2012 with sample data
- Microsoft Visual Studio 2010 with Microsoft Dynamics AX reporting extension
- Microsoft Dynamics SQL Server Reporting Services

Creating a Report Model project

To create a Report Model project, we consider the following steps:

1. Start Visual Studio and press *Ctrl + N* to create a new project.
2. Select **Microsoft Dynamics AX** under **Installed Templates** in the left pane, and select **Report Model**.

3. Provide a name for the project as `SalesAnalysis`.

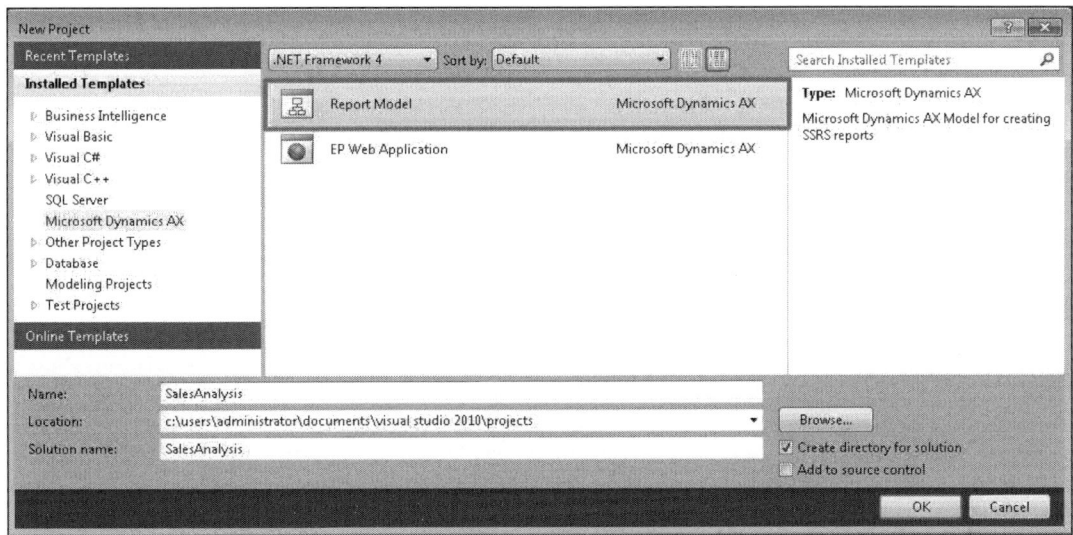

Screenshot 2: New project

Creating a Matrix report using Auto Design

To create a Matrix report using Auto Design, we consider the following steps:

1. Right-click on **Solution**, and select **Report** under the **Add** submenu. Select the report and rename it to `SalesByCustomer`.

2. Right-click on **Datasets** and click on **Add dataset**.

3. Modify the following properties for the newly added dataset:

    1. **Data source** to **Microsoft Dynamics AX**.

    2. **Data source typ**e to **Query**.

    3. **Default Layout** to **Matrix**.

    4. **Name** to **SalesCustByYearDS**.

4. Switch to the **Query** property, and click on the ⬚ button to open the **Query** dialog box.

5. Select **SalesTableListPage** from the list and click on the **Next** button:

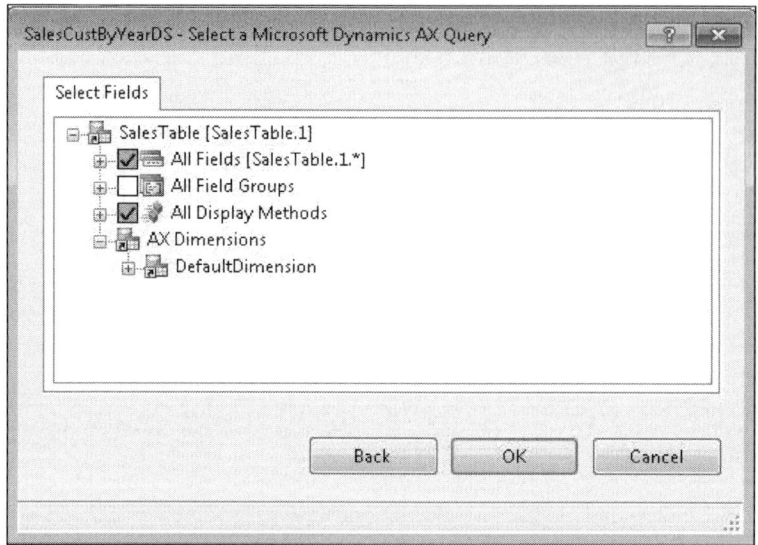

Screenshot 3: New dataset named SalesCustByYearDS

6. Select the **CustAccount**, **createdDateTime** fields from **SalesTable**. Select the **amountInvoiced()** display method and the **customerName**() display method (Refer to Screenshot 3: New Dataset).

7. Locate the **amountInvoiced** field under the **SalesCustByYearDS** dataset.

8. Set the **Aggregation** property to **Sum** and format string to **Currency**.

9. Drag-and-drop **SalesCustByYearDS** to the Design section of the report. This will create a new Auto Design named as **AutoDesign1**.

10. Select **AutoDesign1**, go to **Properties**, and set the following properties:

    1. **LayoutTemplate** to **ReportLayoutStyleTemplate**.
    2. **Title** to `Sales by customer`.

11. Select **SalesCustByYearDS** under **AutoDesign1** and set the following properties:

    1. **StyleTemplate** to **MatrixStyleTemplate**.
    2. **Title** to `Sales by customer matrix`.

12. Under the **Data** node, select only the **amountInvoiced** field.

13. Drag-and-drop **createdDateTime** to column groupings.

14. Select the **createdDateTime** grouping under the column grouping, and change the **Label** property to `=year(Fields!createdDateTime.Value)`.

15. In the model editor, expand **createdDateTime**, expand **Group** on node, select **createdDateTime**, and change the **Expression** property to `=year(Fields!createdDateTime.Value)`.

16. Drag-and-drop **CustAccount** and **customerName** to row groupings.

17. Make the **Display Subtotals** property to **False** for **CustAccount** and the **CustomerName** row grouping.

Saving the report to AOT and deploying it to the Report Server

To save a report to AOT and deploy it to the Report Server, we consider the following steps:

1. In the Solution Explorer, right-click on the **Report Model** project and select **Build**.

2. Once the report is successfully built, right-click on the **Report Model** project and select **Add SalesAnalysis to AOT**.

3. Once the report is added to AOT, we can deploy the same to the Report Server.

4. To deploy the report to the Report Server, consider the following steps:

    1. Right-click on the **Report Model** project and select **Deploy**.

    2. Switch to AOT, right-click on the **SalesByCustomer** report under **AOT | SSRS Reports | Deploy Element**.

5. Deploy using Microsoft Dynamics AX 2012 Management Shell:

    1. Click on **Start | Administrative** tools.

    2. Right-click on **Microsoft Dynamics AX 2012 Management Shell**.

    3. Click on **Run as administrator**.

    4. Enter the following PowerShell command to deploy the report:

```
Publish-AXReport -ReportName SalesByCustomer
```

Running the report

The following steps are performed to run a report:

1. Create an Output menu item by right-clicking on **AOT** and then navigating to **Menu Items | Output | New menu item**.

2. Rename the menu item to `SalesByCustomerMatrix`.

3. Modify the following properties:

   1. **Label** to `Sales by customer`.
   2. **HelpText** to `Sales by customer`.
   3. **ObjectType** to **SSRSReport**.
   4. **Object** to **SalesByCustomer**.
   5. **ReportDesign** to **AutoDesign1**.

4. Save all changes.

5. Right-click on the **SalesByCustomerMatrix** menu item and select **Open**.

6. Provide some dynamics filters if required.

7. Click on **Ok** to run the report:

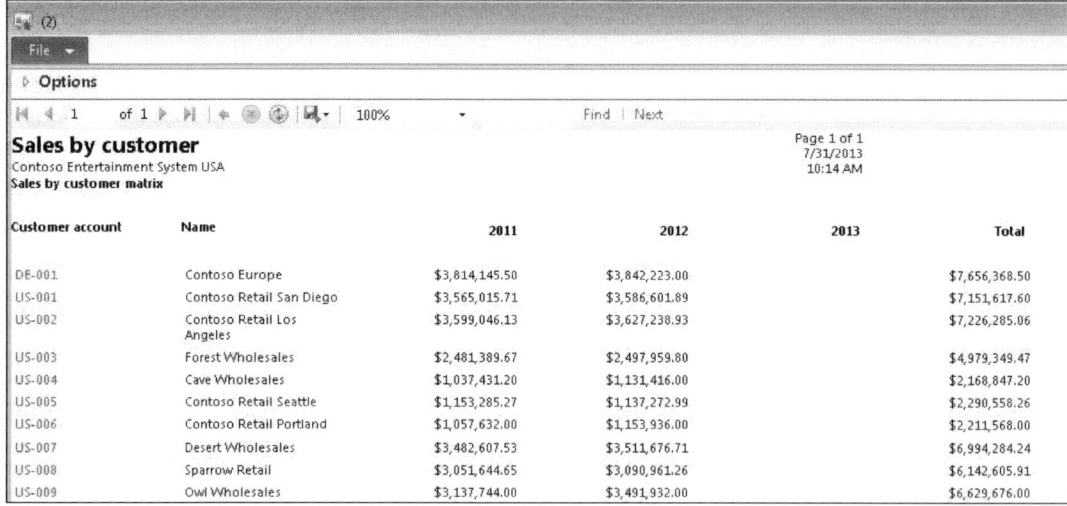

Customer account	Name	2011	2012	2013	Total
DE-001	Contoso Europe	$3,814,145.50	$3,842,223.00		$7,656,368.50
US-001	Contoso Retail San Diego	$3,565,015.71	$3,586,601.89		$7,151,617.60
US-002	Contoso Retail Los Angeles	$3,599,046.13	$3,627,238.93		$7,226,285.06
US-003	Forest Wholesales	$2,481,389.67	$2,497,959.80		$4,979,349.47
US-004	Cave Wholesales	$1,037,431.20	$1,131,416.00		$2,168,847.20
US-005	Contoso Retail Seattle	$1,153,285.27	$1,137,272.99		$2,290,558.26
US-006	Contoso Retail Portland	$1,057,632.00	$1,153,936.00		$2,211,568.00
US-007	Desert Wholesales	$3,482,607.53	$3,511,676.71		$6,994,284.24
US-008	Sparrow Retail	$3,051,644.65	$3,090,961.26		$6,142,605.91
US-009	Owl Wholesales	$3,137,744.00	$3,491,932.00		$6,629,676.00

Screenshot 4: Final report

Walkthrough – Creating a Chart report

Scenario

Steve, a Sales manager, needs to analyze the business sales year, customer group, and country wise. For this, he wants a report which shows graphical comparison of sales made by the business.

This walkthrough illustrates the following tasks:

- Creating an AOT Query
- Creating a Report Model project
- Creating an Auto Design SSRS report
- Saving the report to AOT and deploying it to the Report Server

Prerequisites

To learn and implement the following walkthrough, you must have:

- Microsoft Dynamics AX 2012 with sample data
- Microsoft Visual Studio 2010 with Microsoft Dynamics AX reporting extension
- Microsoft Dynamics SQL Server Reporting Services

Creating an AOT Query

To create an AOT Query, we consider the following steps:

1. Open Microsoft Dynamics AX 2012 from the Start menu.
2. Open the Development Workspace. You can open it by either of the following options:
    1. Press *Ctrl + D* to open AOT in the Development Workspace.
    2. Press *Ctrl + Shift + P* to open **Projects** in the Development Workspace. OR
    3. Press *Alt + W* to open windows and select **New Development Workspace**.
    4. Press *Ctrl + Shift + W* to open **New Development Workspace**.

3. Go to the **AOT | Queries** node.

4. Right-click on the **Queries** node and navigate to **New Query**.

5. Right-click on the newly created query and select **Properties**.

6. Set the following properties:

    1. Provide the name as `SalesCustomerChart`.

    2. Provide the title as `Customer sales chart`.

    3. Provide the descriptions as `Customer sales`.

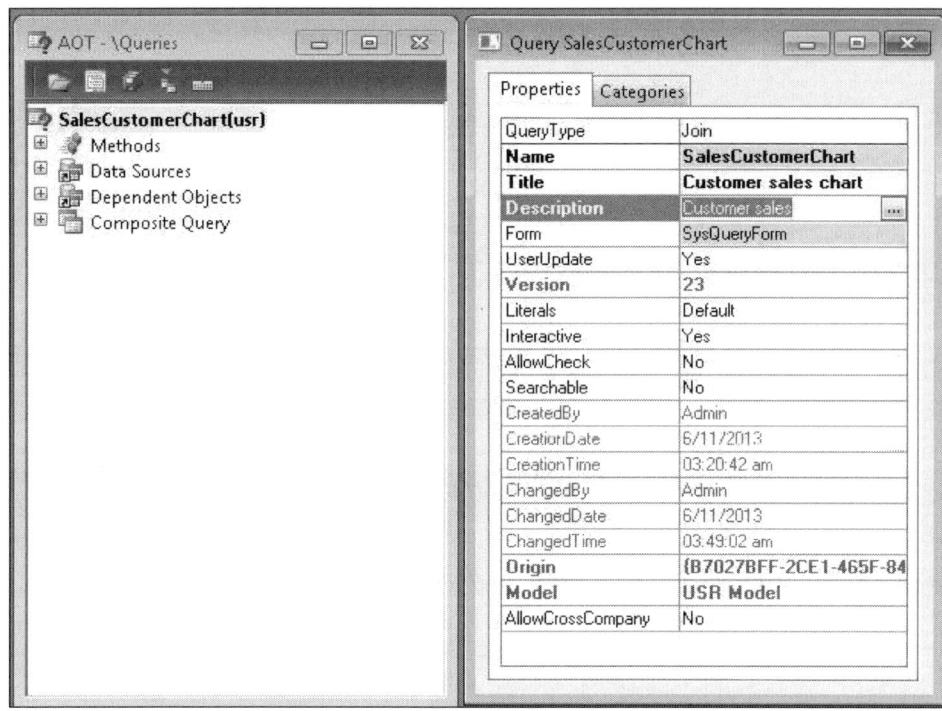

Screenshot 5: Query (SalesCustomerChart)

7. Under **SalesCustomerChart**, right-click on **Data Sources** and select **New Data Source**.

8. Set the **Table** property for the new data source to **SalesTable**.

9. Select the **Fields** node and set the **Dynamic property** to **Yes**.

10. Right-click on the **Data Source** node and select the new data source under **SalesTable_1** data source.

11. Set the **Table** property for the new data source to **CustTable**, and also set the **Relations** property to **Yes**.

12. Select the **Fields** node and set the **Dynamic property** to **No** under **CustTable_1** data source.

13. Right-click on the **Data Source** node and select the new data source under **CustTable_1** data source.

14. Set the **Table** property for the new data source to **CustGroup**, and also set the **Relations** property to **Yes**.

15. Select the **Fields** node and set the Dynamic property to **No** under the **CustGroup _1** data source.

16. Save the query.

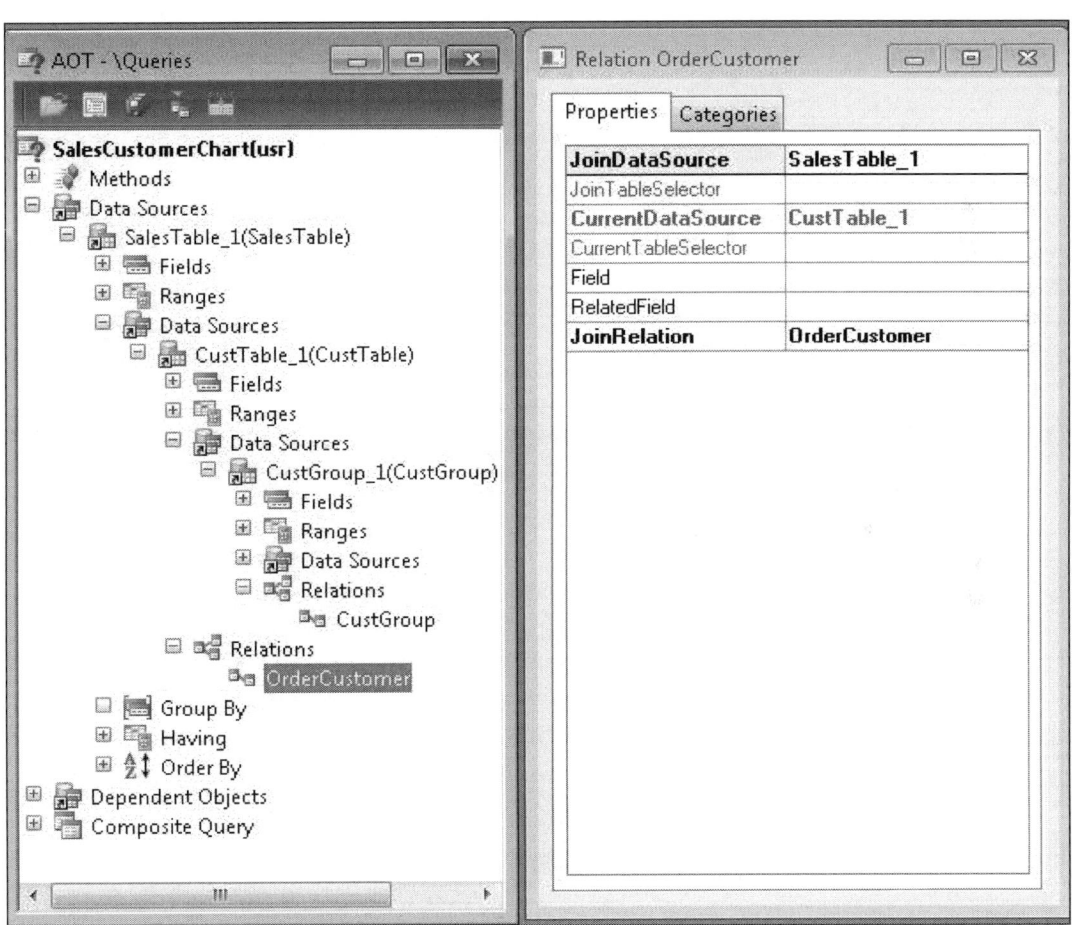

Screenshot 6: AOT Query

Creating a Report Model project

To create a Report Model project, we consider the following steps:

1. Start Visual Studio and press *Ctrl + N* to create a new project.
2. Select Microsoft Dynamics AX under **Installed Templates** in the left pane, and select **Report Model**.
3. Provide a name for the project as `SalesCustomerChart`:

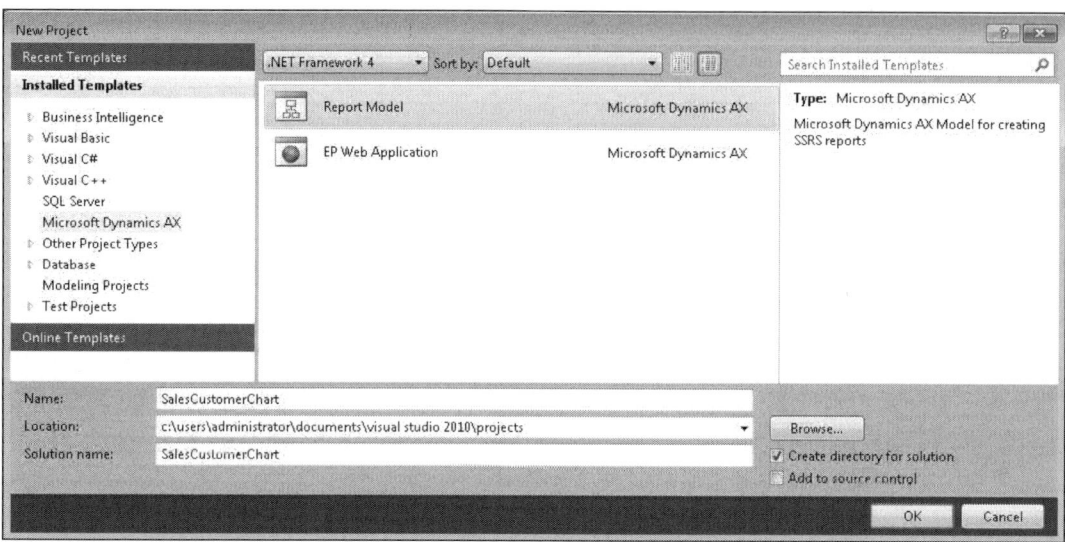

Screenshot 7: New Visual Studio project

Creating an Auto Design SSRS report

To create an Auto Design SSRS report, we consider the following steps:

1. Right-click on **Solution** and select **Report** under the **Add** submenu. Select the report and rename it to `SalesCustomerChart`.
2. Right-click on **Datasets** and click on **Add dataset**.
3. Modify the following properties for the newly added dataset:
    1. **Data source** to **Microsoft Dynamics AX**.
    2. **Data source type** to **Query**.
    3. **Default Layout** to **ColumnChart**.

4. **Name** to `SalesChartDS`.

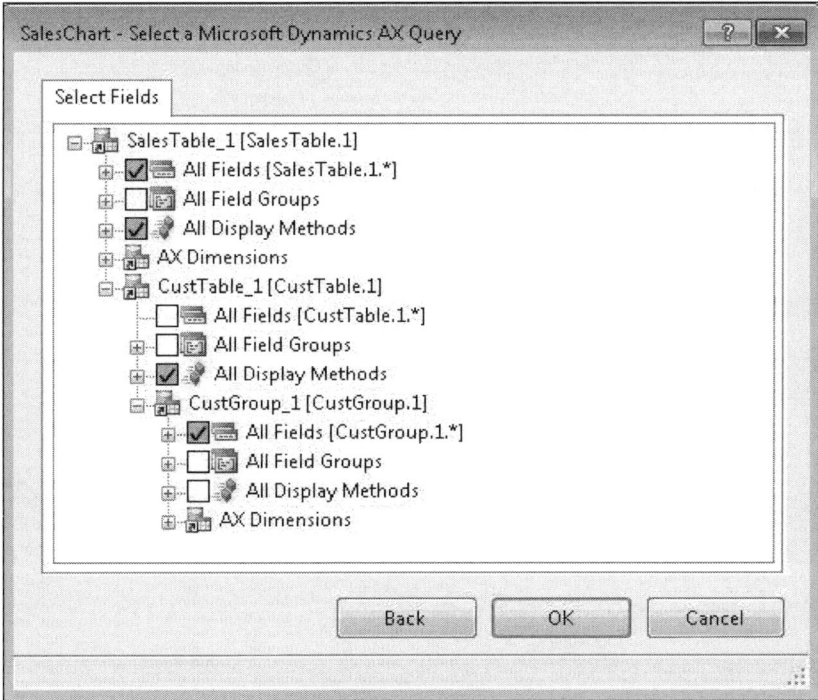

Screenshot 8: New dataset

4. Switch to the **Query property** and click on the button in the right corner to open the **Query** dialog.

5. Select **SalesCustomerChart** from the list and click on the **Next** button.

6. Select the **createdDateTime()**, **amountInvoiced()** display method fields from **SalesTable_1**, select **countryName**() display method from **CustTable_1**, select **CustGroup**, and **Name** from **CustGroup_1** [Refer to Screenshot 8: New Dataset].

7. Locate the **amountInvoiced** field under the **SalesChartDS** dataset.

8. Set the aggregation property to **Sum** and format string to **Currency**.

9. Drag-and-drop **SalesChartDS** to the Design section of the report. This will create a new Auto Design named as **AutoDesign1**.

10. Select **AutoDesign1**, go to **Properties**, and set the following properties:

    1. **LayoutTemplate** to **ReportLayoutStyleTemplate**.

    2. **Title** to Customer sales chart.

11. Select **SalesChartDSXYChart** under **AutoDesign1** and set the following properties:

12. Locate the **Data** node under the **SalesChartDSXYChart** design.

13. Drag-and-drop the **createdDateTime** field to the **Series** node.

14. Change the **createdDateTime** series label to =year(Fields!createdDateTime.Value).

15. Select the **createdDateTime** group under the **createdDateTime** series and change the **Expression** property to =year (Fields!createdDateTime.Value):

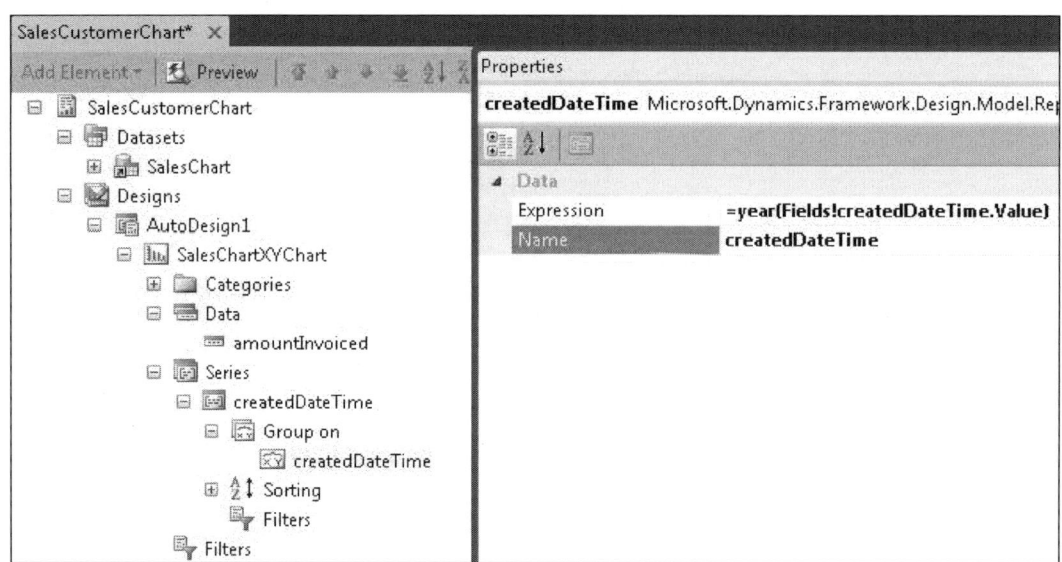

Screenshot 9: Chart series

16. Drag-and-drop the **countryName** and **CustGroup** fields to the **Categories** node.

17. There must not be any field except the **amountInvoiced** under the **Data** node.

18. Save all the changes.

Saving the report to AOT and deploying it to the Report Server

In the Solution Explorer, right-click on the **Report Model** project and select **Build**.

1. Once the report is successfully built, right-click on the **Report Model** project and select **Add SalesCustomerChart to AOT**.

2. Once the report is added to AOT, we can deploy the same to the **Report Server.**

3. To deploy the report to the Report Server:

   1. Right-click on the **Report Model** project and select **Deploy**.

   2. Switch to AOT, right-click on **SalesCustomerChart** report under **AOT | SSRS Reports | Select Deploy Element**.

   3. Deploy using **Microsoft Dynamics AX 2012 Management Shell**.

Deploying using Microsoft Dynamics AX 2012 Management Shell

The deployment can be done using the following steps:

1. Click on **Start | Administrative tools**.

2. Right-click on **Microsoft Dynamics AX 2012 Management Shell**.

3. Click on **Run as administrator**.

4. Enter the following PowerShell command to deploy.

```
Publish-AXReport -ReportName SalesCustomerChart
```

Running the report

1. Create an Output menu item by right-clicking on **AOT | Menu Items | Output | New menu item.**

2. Rename the menu item to `SalesCustomerChart`.

3. Set the following properties:
    1. **Label** to `Sales by customer`.
    2. **HelpText** to `Sales by customer`.
    3. **ObjectType** to **SSRSReport**.
    4. **Object** to **SalesCustomerChart**
    5. **ReportDesign** to **AutoDesign1**

4. Save all changes.

5. Right-click on the **SalesCustomerChart** menu item and select **Open**.

6. Provide some dynamics filters if required.

7. Click on **Ok** to run the report:

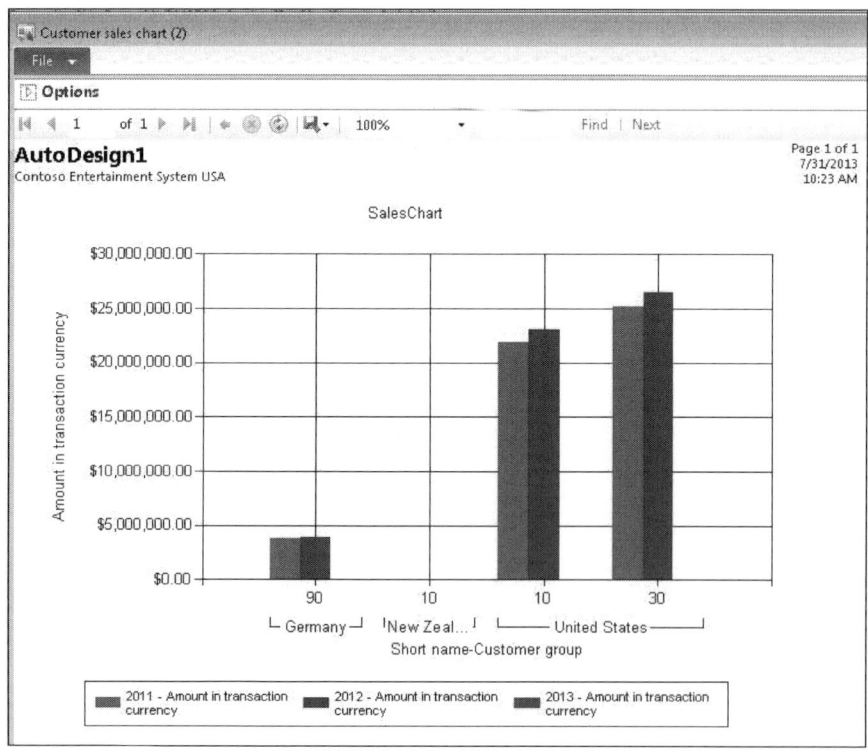

Screenshot 10: Final report

Summary

In this chapter, we learned how to create advance reports for Microsoft Dynamics AX 2012 in Visual Studio. Chart reports are commonly used to compare and contrast large volumes of aggregated information at a glance.

In the next chapter, we learn how to develop reports for Microsoft Dynamics AX 2012 using external data sources.

3
Developing a Report from an External Data Source

In this chapter, we will learn about creating reports for **Microsoft Dynamics AX 2012** using an external data source in Visual Studio. An external data source could be any SQL database where data is hosted by any third party applications, and it has to be rendered in AX. We will also cover the following topics in detail:

- Creating an external data source
- Creating a report using an external data source
- Modifying report appearances

Microsoft Dynamics AX 2012 provides the ability to use a variety of data sources. AX reports can access data from the Microsoft Dynamics AX database, OLAP databases, external OLTP databases, or even C# code. In this chapter, we will learn how to develop Microsoft Dynamics AX reports that access data from an external database, that is independent of Microsoft Dynamics AX.

Walkthrough – Creating a report using an external data source

Scenario

This walkthrough illustrates the following tasks:

- Preparing report data
- Creating a report project
- Creating an external report data source
- Creating a report
- Modifying report appearances

Prerequisites

To learn and implement the following walkthrough, you must have:

- Adventure Works database for SQL 2008 R2
- Microsoft Dynamics AX 2012 with sample data
- Microsoft Visual Studio 2010 with Microsoft Dynamics AX reporting extensions
- Microsoft Dynamics SQL Server Reporting Services

Preparing report data

In order to execute this report, you must download and install the Adventure Works database for SQL 2008 R2.

The Adventure Works database can be downloaded from the following URL:

`http://msftdbprodsamples.codeplex.com/releases/view/93587`

After downloading, perform the following steps to attach `.mdf` and `.ldf` files to the SQL Server database:

1. Click on **Start** | **All Programs** | **SQL Server Management Studio 2008 R2** | **SQL Server Management Studio**.
2. Connect to the respective database server.
3. Right-click on **Databases** | **Attach**.

4. Click on **Add | Browse** and navigate to the directory where the file was downloaded.

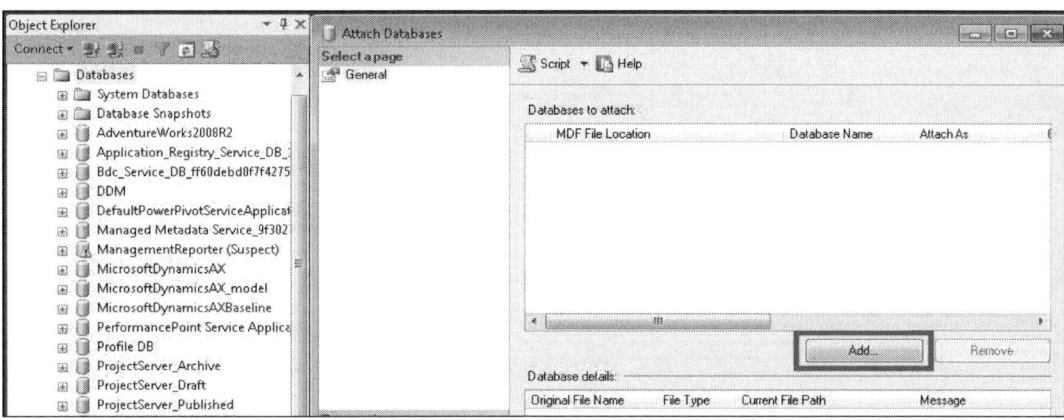

Attaching a database

5. Locate the MDF and LDF files in the file system.

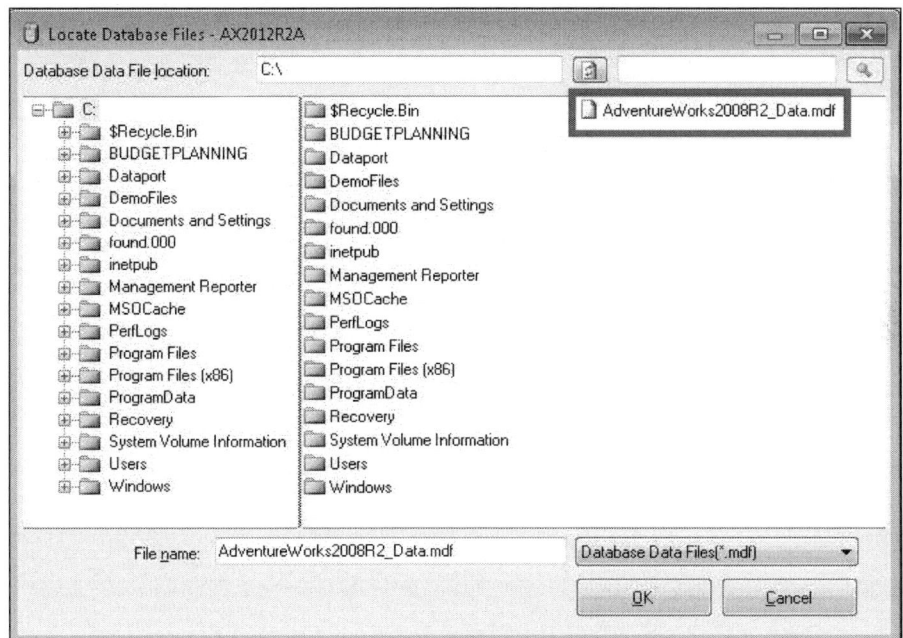

Locating a MDF file

6. Click on **Ok** to select.

7. Click on **Ok** to attach the Adventure Works database, to append to the SQL Server database.

8. Once the Adventure Works database is attached, you can see it under the **Databases** node.

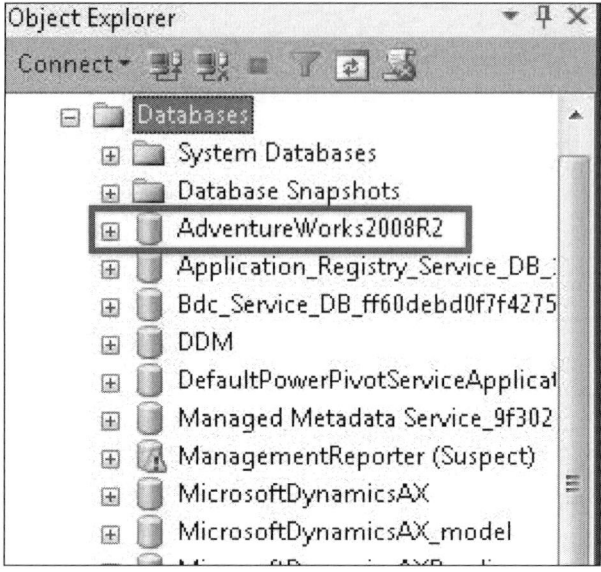

Attaching Database

Creating a report project

1. Start Visual Studio and press *Ctrl + N* to create a new project.

2. Select Microsoft Dynamics AX under **Installed Templates** in the left pane, and select **Report Model**.

3. Provide a name for the project as `SalesByRegion_ExternalDB`.

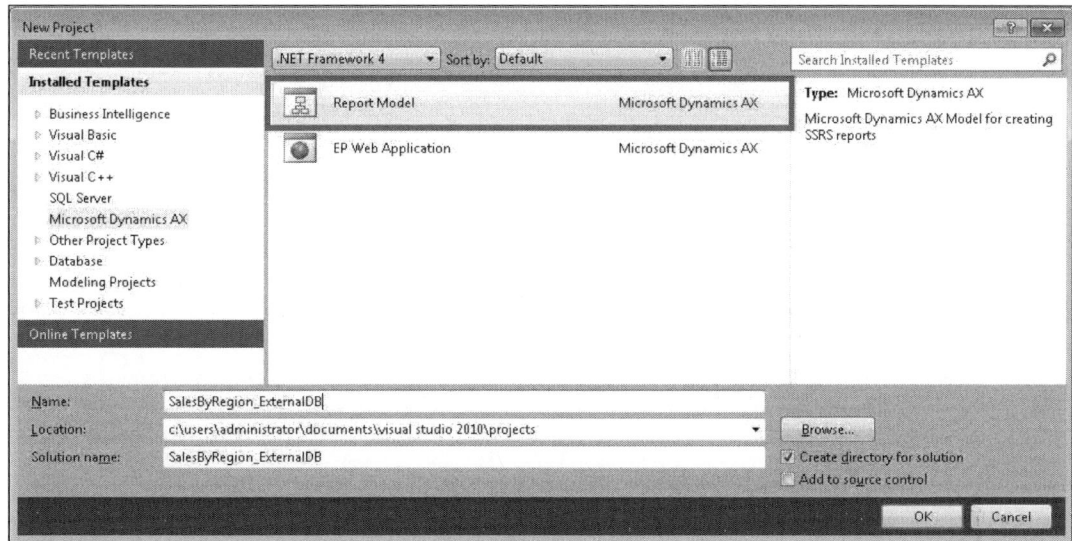

Creating a new project

Creating an external report data source

1. Right-click on the **SalesByRegion_ExternalDB** project in the **Solution Explorer**.

2. Click on **Add | Report data source**.

3. Rename the data source to `SalesByRegionDS`.

Creating reports

1. Right-click on **Solution**, and select **Report** under the **Add** submenu. Select the report and rename the report to `SalesByRegion_ExternalDB`.

2. Right-click on **Datasets** and click on **Add dataset**.

3. Modify the following properties for the newly added dataset:

    1. **Data source** to **SalesByRegionDS**.

    2. **Data source type** to **Query**.

    3. **Default Layout** to **PieChart**.

    4. **Name** to `SalesByRegionDS`.

4. Switch to the **Query** property, and click on the button at the corner to open the **Query** dialog.

5. In the **Query** window, provide the following query:

```
SELECT TOP (5) Name, CountryRegionCode, MAX(SalesYTD) AS
SalesYTD
FROM Sales.SalesTerritory
GROUP BY Name, CountryRegionCode
ORDER BY SalesYTD DESC
```

Downloading the example code

You can download the example code files for all Packt books you have purchased from your account at http://www.packtpub.com. If you purchased this book elsewhere, you can visit http://www.packtpub. com/support and register to have the files e-mailed directly to you.

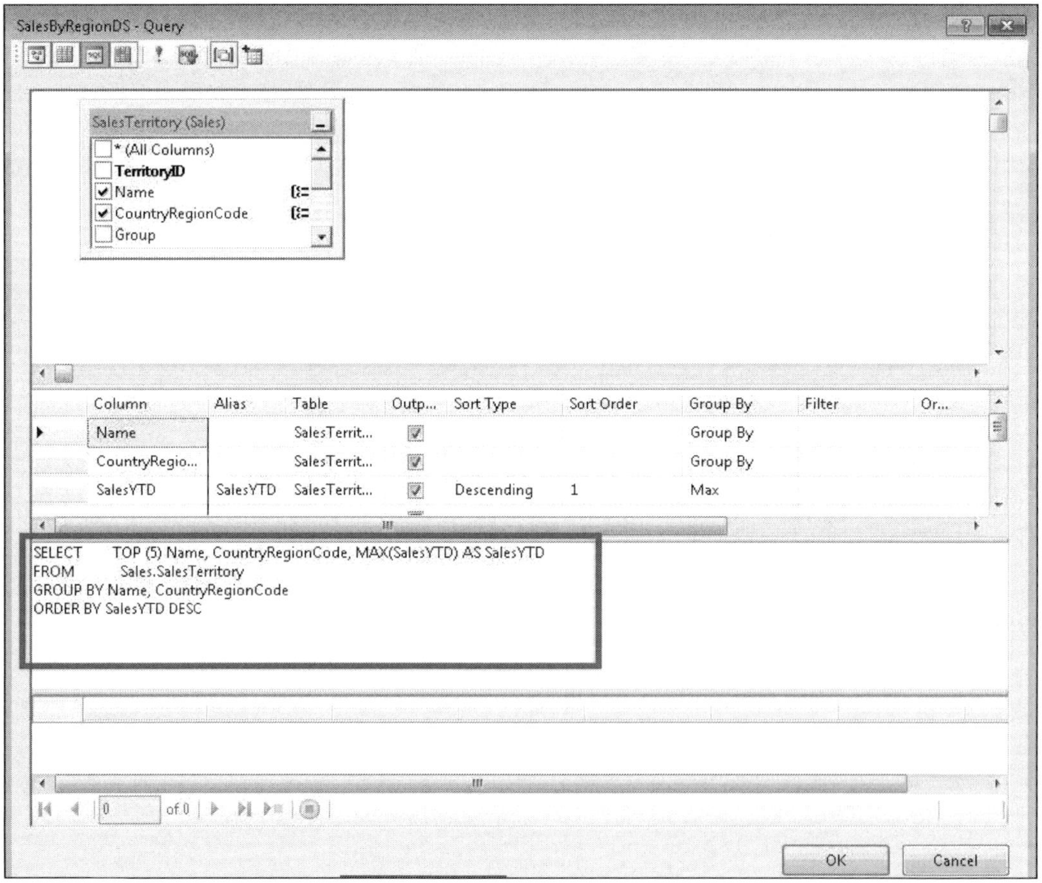

SQL Query

6. Drag-and-drop **SalesByRegionDS** to the Design section of the report; this will create a new Auto Design named as **AutoDesign1**.

Modifying report appearances

1. Select **AutoDesign1**, go to **Properties**, and set the following properties:
    1. **LayoutTemplate** to **ReportLayoutStyleTemplate**.
    2. **Title** to Sales by customer.

2. Select **SalesByRegionDS** under **AutoDesign1**, and set the following properties:
    1. **StyleTemplate** to **PieAndDoughnutChartStyleTemplate**.
    2. **Title** to Sales by region.

3. Under the **Data** node, select the **SalesYTD** field only.

4. Drag-and-drop **Name** and **CountryRegionCode** to the **Series** node.

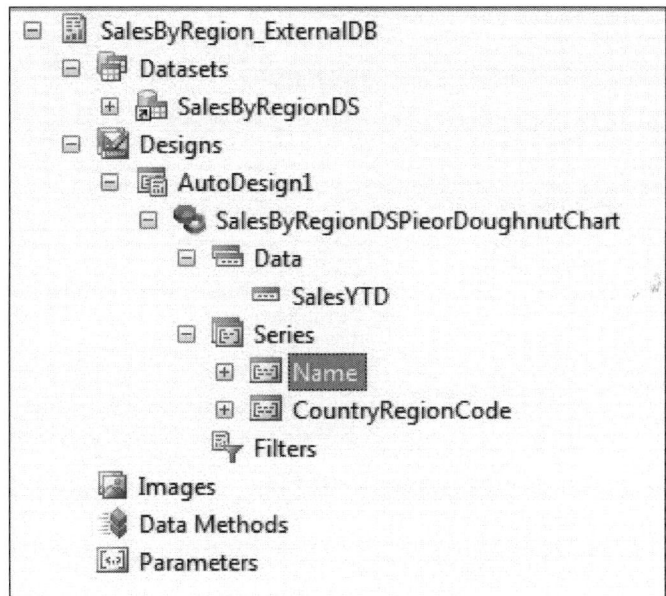

Report design

Report preview

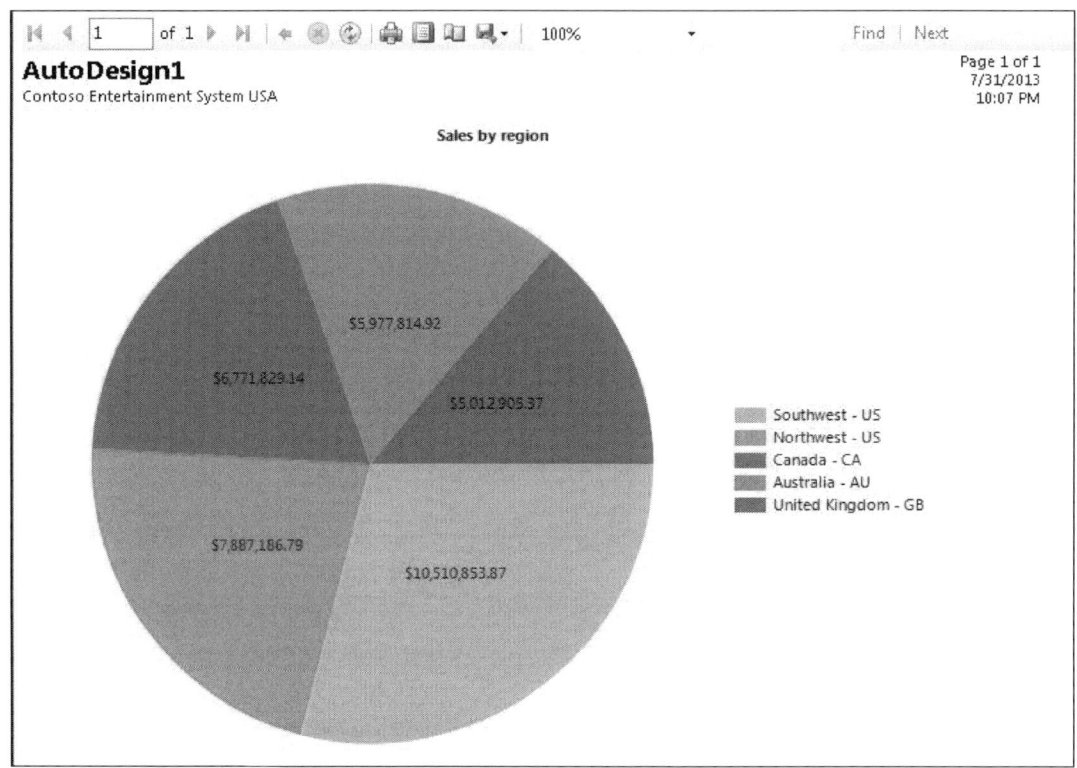

Final report

Summary

In this chapter, we learned how to create a report for Microsoft Dynamics AX 2012 using an external data source. Data coming from an external data source does not pass through **XDS (Extensible Data Security)** layer, so report data can't be secured.

In the next chapter we will learn how to import reports in AX from Visual Studio, and we will also learn about the report deployment process.

4
Importing Reports from Visual Studio to AX and Report Deployment

In this chapter, we will learn managing Microsoft Dynamics AX 2012 Reports inside Visual Studio. Visual Studio is used to create reporting projects, add reports to a project, edit reports, and deploy reports to the Report Server. We'll learn the following topics in detail:

- Edit a Report Model project
- Add reports to a Report Model project
- Import a Report Model project to AOT
- Deploy the report

Microsoft Dynamics AX supports a variety of Visual Studio projects. The Visual Studio Projects node in the AOT contains all the Visual Studio Projects that are part of Microsoft Dynamics AX.

The Dynamics AX Model Project contains the SSRS Report Model Projects that are used for developing reports using Visual Studio. To open **AOT**, press *Ctrl + D* inside AX 2012, and go to the **Visual Studio Projects** tree node. The **Visual Studio Project** tree node holds all projects developed using Visual Project.

Visual Studio Projects in AOT

All the reports developed can be seen under **AOT | SSRS reports | Reports**. There isn't an easy way to identify which report project contains which reports. A detailed list of out-of-the- box reports available in AX 2012 R2 is available at: http://technet.microsoft.com/en-us/library/hh334471.aspx.

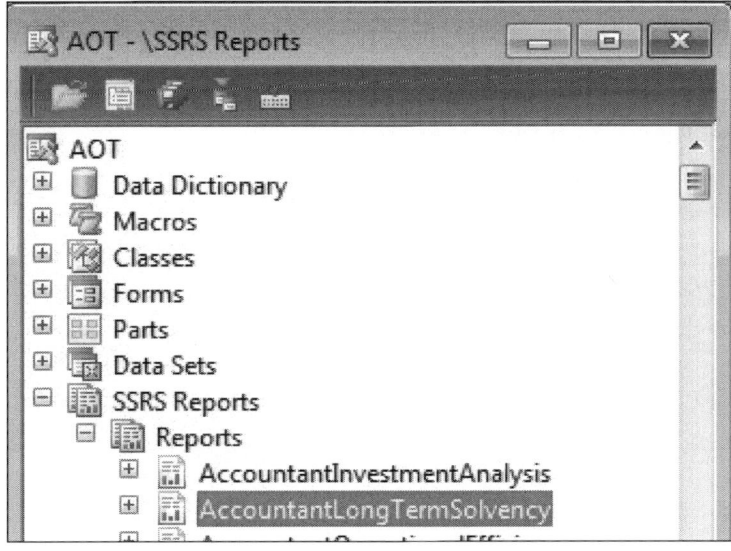

SSRS Reports

Adding a report to Visual Studio Project

1. Open Visual Studio from the Start menu.

2. Press *Ctrl + O* to open the Report Model project from a physical location.

3. Browse to the directory, and select the **Project Solution** file.

4. Click on **Open** to open the solution in Visual Studio.

5. In the Solution Explorer, right-click on the reporting project that you want to add a report to, and then click on **Add Report**.

Alternatively, if you want to edit the project from AOT, perform the following steps:

1. Open Microsoft Dynamics AX 2012 from the Start menu.

2. Go to **AOT | Visual Studio Projects | Dynamics AX Model Projects**.

3. Select the project to be edited and right-click on the same, and navigate to **Edit**.

Adding a report project to the AOT

1. Open a Report Model project by following the preceding steps in Microsoft Visual Studio.

2. Click on **View | Solution Explorer**, right-click on the project, and click on **Add [ReportProjectName] to AOT**. The report design will be added to AOT.

Report deployment

Microsoft Dynamics AX 2012 provides a variety of mechanisms for deploying reports to SQL Server Reporting Services Report Server (SRSS).

Microsoft Dynamics AX

We can deploy SSRS Reports to the Report Server from AOT by performing the following steps:

1. Navigate to the **AOT | SSRS Reports | Reports** node.

2. Select report/reports to be deployed.

3. Right-click and select **Deploy Element**.

Microsoft Visual Studio

We can deploy the SSRS reports to the Report Server from Visual Studio by performing the following steps:

4. Open **Dynamics AX Model Project** in Visual Studio

5. Click on **View | Solution Explorer**, right-click on the project, and select **Deploy**.

Microsoft Dynamics AX 2012 Management Shell

Reports can be deployed to the Report Server from the PowerShell by performing the following steps:

1. Click on **Start | Administrative Tools**.

2. Right-click on the **Microsoft Dynamics AX 2012 Management Shell** option

3. Click on **Run as administrator**.

4. Type the following command to deploy the report. For example, let's deploy the **CustTransList** report:

```
Publish-AXReport -ReportName CustTransList
```

To deploy multiple reports using PowerShell, we can use the following command:

```
Publish-AXReport -ReportName Sales, SalesAnalysis
```

To deploy all the reports using PowerShell, we can use the following command:

```
Publish-AXReport -ReportName *
```

To deploy reports to a different Report Server, we can use the following command:

```
Publish-AXReport - ReportName <String> -ServiceAOSName
<String> -ServicesAOSWSDLPort <Int32>
```

To learn more about Windows PowerShell, you can refer to the following link: http://technet.microsoft.com/en-us/library/hh272856.aspx.

Summary

In this chapter we learned how to edit report projects and reports available in Microsoft Dynamics AX 2012. We also learned about how to save projects back to AOT and deploy reports to the Report Server.

In the next chapter, we will learn how to design complex SSRS reports using Report Controller and UI Builder classes for Microsoft Dynamics AX 2012.

5
Using Controller and User Interface Builder Classes

In this chapter, we will learn about developing reports using controller and user interface classes. The `controller` class gives flexibility to control the behavior of the report before running the report, and the `user interface` class is used to develop a user interface which is prompted to the end users while running a report. We will also study the following topics:

- The Model-View-Controller (MVC) pattern in Reporting
- The `Report controller` class
- The `UI Builder` class

Microsoft SQL Server Reporting Services (SSRS) is the primary reporting framework for Microsoft Dynamics AX 2012. AX Reporting Framework is based on the MVC design pattern.

The Model-View-Controller

MVC is a pattern which is used to isolate business logic from the user interface. The MVC design pattern is based on the following three key pillars:

Model

Model is responsible for executing all the business logic and retrieving data using complex queries, data methods, or classes performing the same.

View

View is responsible for rendering the data to the users' screen in a well formatted pattern.

Controller

Controller controls communication between the Model and the View.

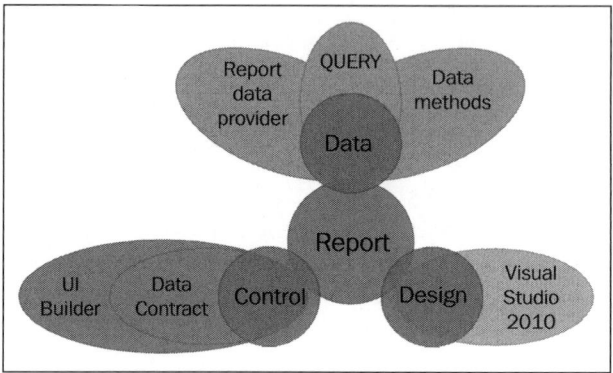

Model-View-Controller design pattern

MVC for Dynamics AX Reporting is based on four main concepts:

- Controller
- UI Builder
- **Report data provider (RDP)** (we will learn this in the next chapter)
- **Report Definition Language (RDL)** contract (we will learn this in the next chapter)

The Controller class

The `Controller` class acts as the controller of the Model-View-Controller design pattern. In AX, the controller role is played by the `SrsReportRunController` class. The `Controller` class performs the following activities:

- Calls `SrsReportRunInterface` to parse RDL
- Gets report contracts
- Creates necessary UI Builders and invokes them

- Call to validate on contracts
- Saves to the SysLastValue table

The Controller class must be overridden in the following mentioned scenarios:

- Change contracts before running a report. For example, to change the query based on the parameters in the form. For this, the modifyReportContract method is used.
- React to form controls events. For this, override methods/events are used.
- Add validations which are not part of the contract class or report data tables. For this, override the validate method and call the super method.
- Change the report name or design based on parameters to add capabilities of rendering multiple reports or multiple report designs using the same reporting controller.
- Changing the company or culture based on parameters. For this, override the modifyReportContract method, and set the company and culture on SrsReportRdlontract.

The Syntax is as follows:

```
public class SrsReportRunController extends SysOperationController
{

}
```

This class handles report rendering and running the report. It takes the report name as a parameter and behaves like the controller to render the UI, react to events, and run SQL Server Reporting Services to display the report.

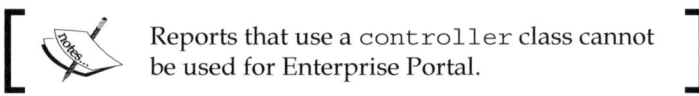 Reports that use a controller class cannot be used for Enterprise Portal.

Please refer to the code of the sample Controller class in the code bundle.

The UI Builder class

UI Builders define how the report run dialog will look. Using the UI Builder class, we can easily customize the look and feel which is to be presented to the end user before running the report.

By using the UI Builder class, we can perform the following activities:

- Add any type of fields over the report dialog
- Enable/disable fields on the basis of other dialog field values
- Add multiple groups under multiple columns
- Add lookups to fields
- Validate input values and so on
- Transfer dialog field values to the report contract

UI Builder uses two main classes: SrsReportDataContractUIBuilder and SysOperationAutomaticUIBuilder.

The SrsReportDataContractUIBuilder class

This class provides the capability to show the date effective tab and validate values that are specified in the report.

```
public class SrsReportDataContractUIBuilder extends SysOperationAutomaticUIBuilder
{

}
```

The framework provides the default UI Builder for every report. You may extend the UI Builder class to add events, create a custom lookup, create custom controls, or change the layout of the parameter form.

You can create grouping; vertical or horizontal alignment, change the number of columns, or add lookups. The following methods can be overridden to add the necessary functionality:

- SrsReportDataContractUIBuilder.addDialogField
- SrsReportDataContractUIBuilder.getFromDialog
- SrsReportDataContractUIBuilder.build
- SrsReportDataContractUIBuilder.buildGroup
- SrsReportDataContractUIBuilder.postrun

The SysOperationAutomaticUIBuilder class

This class provides capabilities to render UI for a given data contract using `SysOperationFramework`.

```
public class SysOperationAutomaticUIBuilder extends SysOperationUIBuilder
{

}
```

Please refer to the code of sample the `UI Builder` class in the code bundle.

Summary

In this chapter, we learned how the Model-View-Controller pattern has been implemented in AX Reporting. Furthermore, we learned the basics of Report Controller and report UI Builder classes. These classes are very useful while creating advance reports in Microsoft Dynamics AX 2012.

In the next chapter, we will learn about Report Contract and Report data provider classes.

6
Developing Reports Using RDP and Report Contracts

In this chapter, we will learn about developing reports using the `Report data provider` class and Report contracts. We will also learn the following topics in detail:

- The `Report contract` class
- The `Report data provider` class
- Developing a report using Report data provider (RDP)
- Creating a Precision Design report
- Creating a report with parameters using the `contract` class

Reporting in Microsoft Dynamics AX 2012 has rapidly changed; lot of new functionalities have been released which have provided a very strong reporting framework to AX 2012. A major change in AX 2012 Reporting Framework is the added capabilities of the Model-View-Controller framework, which we studied in the preceding chapter.

In this chapter, we will learn about the Report data provider and the Report contract classes.

The Report data provider class

A Report data provider class is commonly known as RDP. RDP is the data source type which is available when we add a new dataset to the report in Visual Studio. RDP is a class which resides inside AX and executes the business logic, processes the data, and returns a dataset which is rendered in the report. A Report data provider class should be ideally used in the following cases:

* We cannot directly use a query to access the data from the database
* The data has to prepare on the basis of business logic

To define a Report data provider class, we use the following syntax:

```
\Classes\SrsRdpTestClass - Editor

classDeclaration          public class SrsRdpTestClass extends SRSReportDataProviderBase
                          {
                                TmpCustTableSample tmpCust;
                          }
```

Sample RDP

The Report contract class

Report contracts in AX 2012 are used for defining parameters to the SSRS report. We can define any number of parameters using X++ statements of any data type, which can be passed on to the RDP class. And then, we can use the same contracts to query data from the database engine which will decrease an overhead on execution of a query in SQL.

To define a Report contract class we use the following syntax:

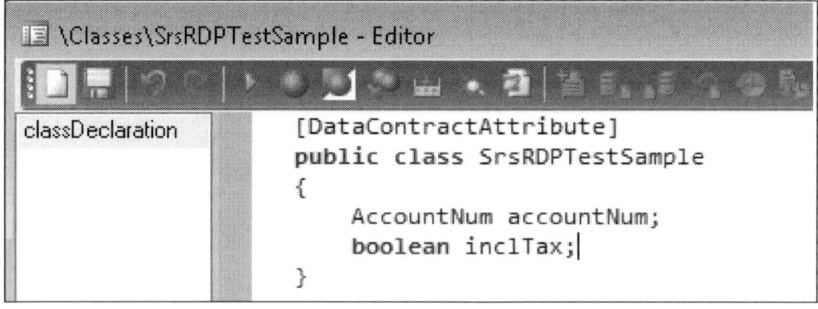

```
\Classes\SrsRDPTestSample - Editor

classDeclaration          [DataContractAttribute]
                          public class SrsRDPTestSample
                          {
                                AccountNum accountNum;
                                boolean inclTax;
                          }
```

Report Contract

Walkthrough – Creating an Auto Design report using the RDP class

Scenario

Matt, a Sales manager, needs a report to analyze total sales for customers.

This walkthrough illustrates the following tasks:

- Creating a Report data provider class
- Creating a Report Model project
- Creating a Table report using Auto Design
- Saving to AOT, deploying, and running the report

Prerequisites

To learn and implement the following walkthrough, you must have:

- Microsoft Dynamics AX 2012 with sample data
- Microsoft Visual Studio 2010 with Microsoft Dynamics AX reporting extension
- Microsoft Dynamics AX 2012 SQL Server Reporting Services

Creating a Report data provider class

1. Open Microsoft Dynamics AX 2012 from the Start menu.
2. Open the development workspace. You can do it in either of the following ways:
    1. Press *Ctrl + D* to open AOT in Development Workspace.
    2. Press *Ctrl + Shift + P* to open Projects in Development Workspace.
    3. Press *Alt + W* to open windows and select **New Development Workspace**.
    4. Press *Ctrl + Shift + W* to open New Development Workspace.
3. Navigate to the **AOT | Classes** node.
4. Right-click on the **Classes** node, and click on **New | Class**.

5. Double-click on the class created and change the class declaration, as shown in the following code:

```
class SrsRDPSample extends SRSReportDataProviderBase{
    CustTransTotalSales custTransTotalSales;
}
```

6. Right-click on the **SrsRDPSample** class and select **New** | **Method**.

7. Modify the method, as shown in the following code:

```
[SRSReportDataSetAttribute('CustSales')]
public CustTransTotalSales getTmpCustTable(){
    return custTransTotalSales;
}
```

8. Right-click on the **SrsRDPSample** class and navigate to **Override method** | **processReport**.

9. Modify the method, as shown in the following code:

```
public void processReport(){
    select * from custTransTotalSales;
}
```

Creating a Report Model project

1. Start Visual Studio and press *Ctrl + N* to create a new project.

2. Select Microsoft Dynamics AX under **Installed Templates** from the left pane, and select **Report Model**.

3. Provide a name for the project as `CustomerTotalSales_Autodesign`.

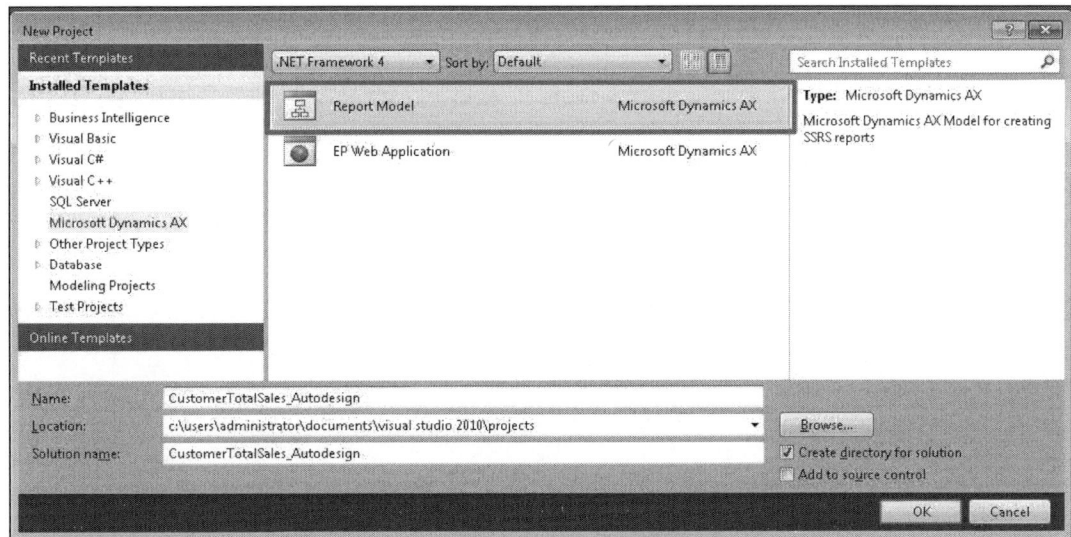

New project

Creating a Table report using Auto Design

1. Right-click on **Solution**, select **Report** under the **Add** submenu. Select the report and rename it to `CustTotalSales_Autodesign`.

2. Right-click on **Datasets** and click on **Add dataset**.

3. Modify the following properties for the newly added dataset:

    1. **Data source** to **Microsoft Dynamics AX**.

    2. **Data source type** to **Query**.

    3. **Default Layout** to **Matrix**.

    4. **Name** to `CustTotalSalesDS`.

4. Switch to the `Query` property, and click on the button besides the name of the entity button to open the Query dialog.

5. Select `SrsRDPSample` from the list and click on the Next button.

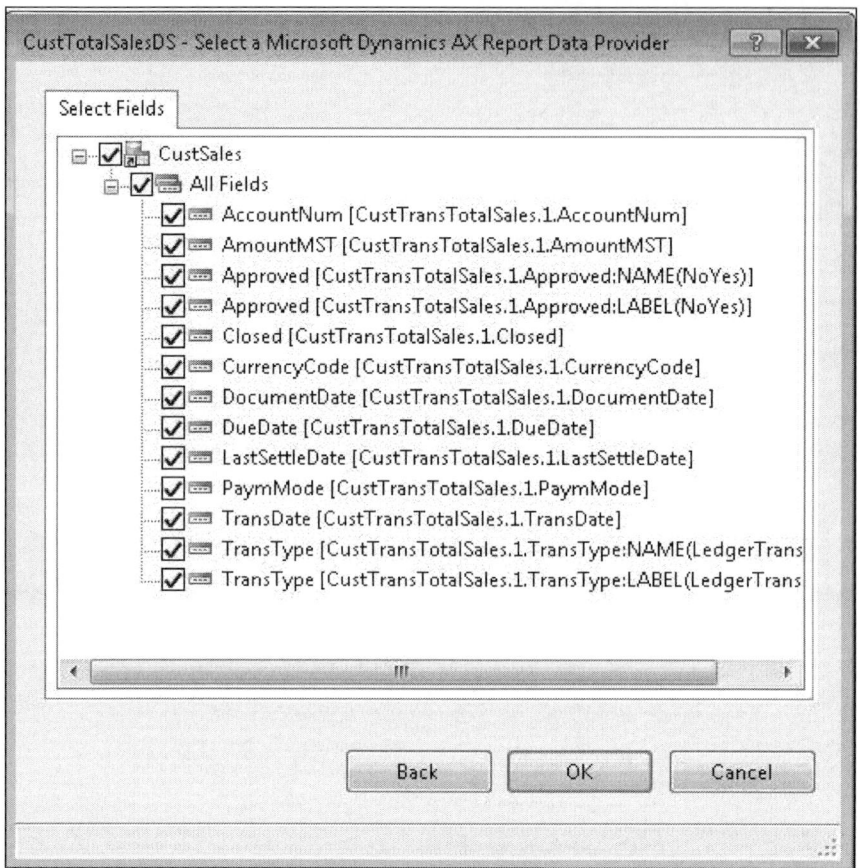

New dataset: CustTotalSalesDS

6. Select all fields from **CustSales**.

7. Drag-and-drop **CustTotalSalesDS** to the Design section of the report. This will create a new Auto Design named as **AutoDesign1**.

8. Select **AutoDesign1**, go to **Properties**, and set the following properties:

    1. **LayoutTemplate** to **ReportLayoutStyleTemplate**

    2. **Title** to `Customer sales`.

9. Select **CustTotalSalesDS** under **AutoDesign1**, and set the
   following properties:

   1. **StyleTemplate** to **TableStyleAlternatingRowsTemplate**.

   2. **Title** to Customer sales.

10. Drag the **AccountNum** field from the **Data** node to **Groupings**.

11. Drag the **TransDate** field to the **Sorting** node.

12. Under the **Data** node, select only the **TransDate**, **AmountMST**,
    CurrencyCode, **DocumentDate**, **DueDate**, **LastSettleDate**, **PaymMode**,
    and **TransType1** fields.

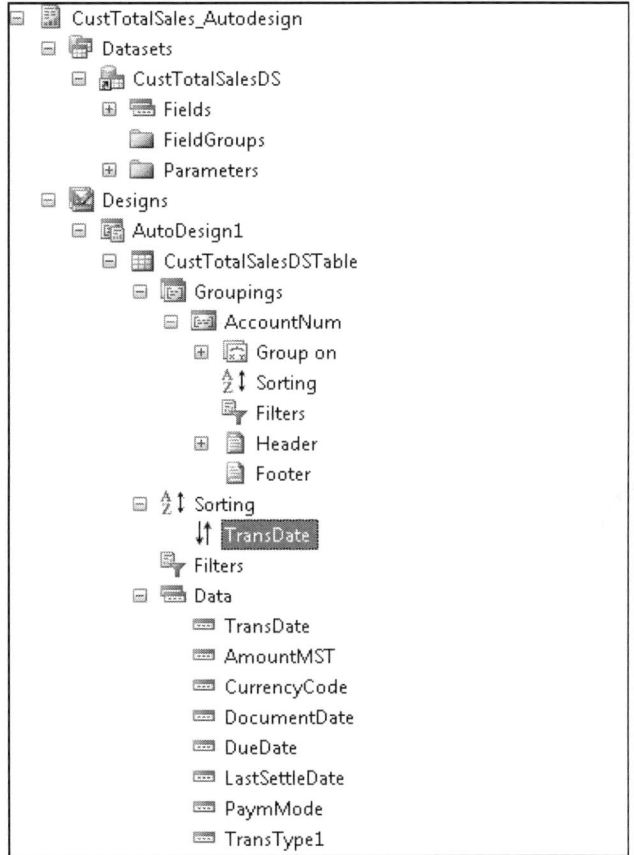

Report design

Saving to AOT, deploying, and running the report

Save the report to AOT and Deploy to the Report Server as explained in previous chapters, and then run the report.

Walkthrough – Creating a Precision Design report

Scenario

Matt—the sales manager, in addition to the report developed in the previous walkthrough wants totals to be printed in the report. Also, he wants that every customer record should start from a new page.

This walkthrough illustrates the following tasks:

- Creating a Precision Design from Auto Design
- Adding totals to the Amount field
- Adding a page break for each customer
- Saving to AOT, deploying and running the report

Creating a Precision Design from Auto Design

To create a Precision Design, perform the following actions:

1. Right-click on **Autodesign1** and click on **Create Precision Design**.
2. Precision Design will be created and will be opened in the New Design window.

Adding totals to the Amount field

1. Right-click on **AccountNum_0** under Row Groupings and select **Add total | after**.

Adding a page break for each customer

1. Right-click on **AccountNum_0** under Row Groupings, and select **Group Properties**.

2. Select the **Page Breaks** tab.

3. Check the **Between each instance of a group** option.

4. Check the **Also at the end of a group** option.

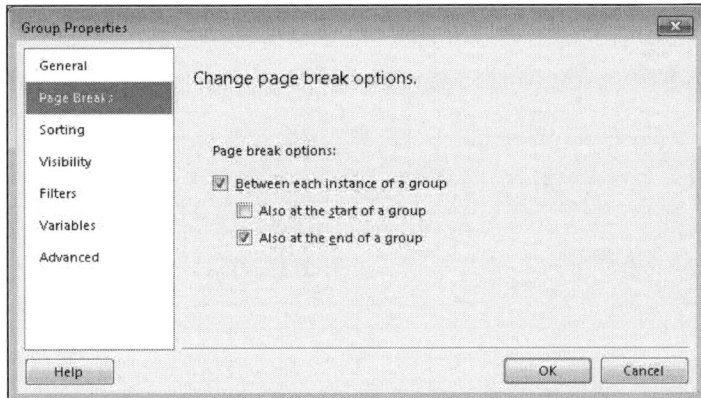

Page breaks (Group)

Saving to AOT, deploying, and running the report

Save the report to AOT and deploy it to the Report Server, as explained in the previous chapters, and then run the report.

Walkthrough: Creating a report with parameters

Scenario

Matt—the sales manager, in addition to the report developed in the previous walkthrough wants to fetch transactions between a specific date range for a specific customer.

This walkthrough illustrates the following tasks:

- Creating a `contract` class
- Modifying RDP to accept the Report Contracts
- Refreshing the Report Dataset for new parameters
- Saving to AOT, deploying, and running the report

Prerequisites

To learn and implement the following walkthrough, you must have:

- Microsoft Dynamics AX 2012 with sample data
- Microsoft Visual Studio 2010 with Microsoft Dynamics AX reporting extension
- Microsoft Dynamics SQL Server Reporting Services

Creating a contract class

1. Open Microsoft Dynamics AX 2012 from the Start menu.
2. Open the development workspace. You can open it by using one of the following options:
    1. Press *Ctrl + D* to open AOT in Development Workspace.
    2. Press *Ctrl + Shift + P* to open Projects in the Development Workspace.
    3. Press *Alt + W* to open windows and select **New Development Workspace**.
    4. Press *Ctrl + Shift + W* to open **New Development Workspace**.

3. Navigate to the **AOT | Classes** node.

4. Right-click on the **Classes** node and navigate to **New | Class**.

5. Double-click on the class created and change the class declaration, as shown in the following code:

```
[DataContractAttribute]
class SrsContractSample{
    AccountNum accountNum;
    FromDate fromDate;
    ToDate toDate;
}
```

6. Right-click on the **SrsContractSample** class and select **New | Method**.

7. Modify the method, as shown in the following code:

```
[DataMemberAttribute("AccountNum")]
public AccountNum parmAccountNum(AccountNum _accountNum =
    accountNum){
    accountNum = _accountNum;
    return accountNum;
}
```

8. Right-click on the **SrsContractSample** class and select **New | Method**.

9. Modify the method, as shown in the following code:

```
[DataMemberAttribute("FromDate")]
public FromDate parmFromDate(FromDate _fromDate =
    fromDate){
    fromDate = _fromDate;
    return fromDate;
}
```

10. Right-click on the **SrsContractSample** class and select **New | Method**.

11. Modify the method, as shown in the following code:

```
[DataMemberAttribute("toDate")]
public toDate parmtoDate(toDate _toDate = toDate){
    toDate = _toDate;
    return toDate;
}
```

Modifying RDP to accept the Report Contracts

1. Go to the **AOT | Classes | SrsRDPSample** class.

2. Modify the class declaration, as shown in the following code:

```
[SRSReportParameterAttribute(classstr(SrsContractSample))]
class SrsRDPSample extends SRSReportDataProviderBase{
   CustTransTotalSales custTransTotalSales;
}
```

> We need to provide a reference of the Contract class to the RDP class so that all the parameters can be mapped with the report data.
>
> To add a reference, we add the SRSReportParameterAttribute attribute in the class declaration.

3. Once the RDP class is attached with the Contract class, we can call the contracts and fetch the data with filters. To perform the same, check the following code:

```
public void processReport(){
   SrsContractSample contract = this.parmDataContract();
   select * from custTransTotalSales
   where custTransTotalSales.AccountNum ==
   contract.parmAccountNum()
   && custTransTotalSales.TransDate >=
   contract.parmFromDate()
   && custTransTotalSales.TransDate <= contract.parmtoDate()
   && custTransTotalSales.TransType ==
   LedgerTransType::Sales;
}
```

Refreshing the Report Dataset for new parameters

1. Right-click on **AOT | Visual Studio Projects | Dynamics AX Model Projects | CustomerTotalSales_Autodesign** and select **Edit**.

2. Browse to the **Report Dataset**.

3. Right-click on the CustTotalSalesDS dataset and select **Refresh**.

4. In the report parameters, you would be able to see the newly added parameters:

    ◦ `CustTotalSalesDS_CustAccount`

    ◦ `CustTotalSalesDS_FromDate`

    ◦ `CustTotalSalesDS_ToDate`

5. Save the report.

Saving to AOT, deploying, and running the report

Save the report to AOT and deploy to the Report Server, as explained in the previous chapters, and then run the report.

Summary

In this chapter, we learned how to develop reports using Report Contracts with Report data provider as the report data source. We also developed the Auto Design and the Precision Design reports.

In the next chapter, we will learn how to customize existing reports available in Microsoft Dynamics AX 2012 using Visual Studio.

7
Customizing Existing Microsoft Dynamics AX Reports Using Visual Studio

Microsoft Dynamics AX 2012 R2 is shipped with more than 800 out-of-the-box reports (Rich client and Role center reports). At various stages of implementation, many out-of-the-box report customizations are required to be made. In this chapter, we will learn how to edit or customize out-of-the-box reports using Visual Studio, save them back to AOT so that they can be shipped with various AX builds, and how to deploy reports after making changes. In addition to this, we'll learn about the following topics in detail:

- How to edit reports in Visual Studio
- Saving changes to AX
- Deploying to the Report Server
- Enabling sorting in an existing report
- Adding new parameters to an existing report

Customizing reports in Microsoft Dynamics AX 2012 has been made very easy. Now, developers can directly edit any of the out-of-the-box or customized SSRS reports projects from AOT, and perform the required modifications.

In this chapter, we will learn several methods to edit reports in different scenarios.

Editing existing reports in Visual Studio

This scenario will cover the following topics:

- Finding and editing a SSRS Report Model Project in AOT
- Saving changes to AX
- Deploying changes to the Report Server

Finding the SSRS Report Model Project in AOT

To find the SSRS Report Model Project in AOT, we perform the following steps:

1. Open Microsoft Dynamics AX 2012 from the Start menu.
2. Open the Development Workspace. You can open it by any of the following methods:
   1. Press *Ctrl + D* to open AOT in the Development Workspace.
   2. Press *Ctrl + Shift + P* to open Projects in Development Workspace.
   3. Press *Alt + W* to open windows and select **New Development Workspace**.
   4. Press *Ctrl + Shift + W* to open **New Development Workspace**.
3. Go to the **AOT | Visual Studio Projects | Dynamics AX Model Projects** node.

4. Find your report project and right-click and select **Edit**.

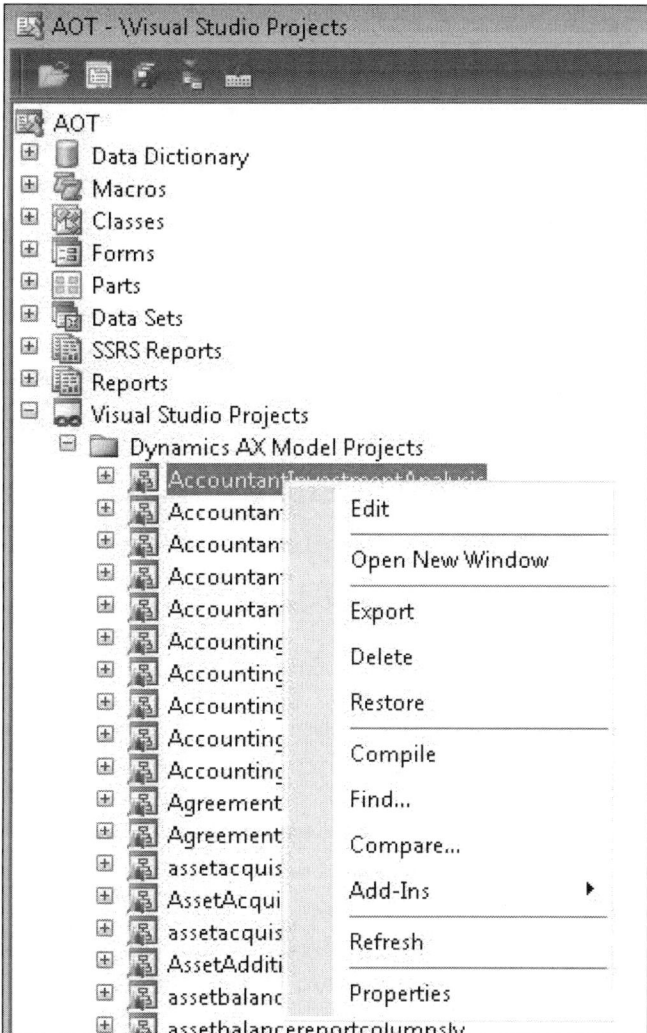

Report Model project

- Once the report is opened in Visual Studio, we can perform the changes as required.

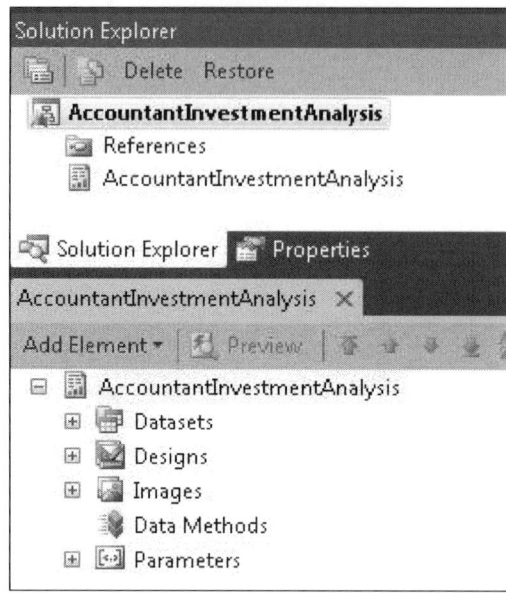

Report in Edit mode: Visual Studio

Saving changes to AX

The steps to perform to save changes to AX are as follows:

1. In the Solution Explorer, right-click on the Report Model project and select **Build**.
2. Once the report is successfully built, right-click on the Report Model project and select **Add AccountantInvestmentAnalysis** to AOT.
3. Reports can be deployed to the Report Server once they are added to AOT.

Deploying changes to the Report Server

1. To deploy a report to the Report Server, we perform the following steps:
2. Right-click on the Report Model project and select **Deploy**.
3. Switch to AOT, right-click on **AccountantInvestmentAnalysis** report under **AOT | SSRS Reports | Select Deploy Element**.

4. Deploy it using Microsoft Dynamics AX 2012 Management Shell. We perform the with the help of the following steps:

   1. Click on **Start** | **Administrative tools**.
   2. Right-click on Microsoft Dynamics AX 2012 Management Shell.
   3. Click on Run as administrator.
   4. Enter the following `PowerShell` command to deploy:

      ```
      Publish-AXReport -ReportName AccountantInvestmentAnalysis
      ```

Enabling a sort order for Sales order ID

Tom, a Sales manager, wants an "Order lines not posted" report available under **Accounts Receivable** | **Reports** | **Transactions** | **Sales Orders** to have a sorting on Sales order ID.

To do so, we perform the following steps:

1. Open Microsoft Visual Studio 2010 from the Start menu.
2. Click on **View** | **Application Explorer**.
3. Browse for the **SalesNotInvoiced** report under **AOT** | **SSRS reports** | **Reports**.
4. Right-click on the report and click on **Edit**.
5. Browse to the report design.
6. Right-click on the report design named **Report** and select **Edit using Designer**.
7. Under row groups, right-click on **Group2 (Sales Id)** and select **Group properties**.
8. Switch to the **Sorting** tab and click on the **Add** button.

9. Select **SalesId** in the **SortBy** column.

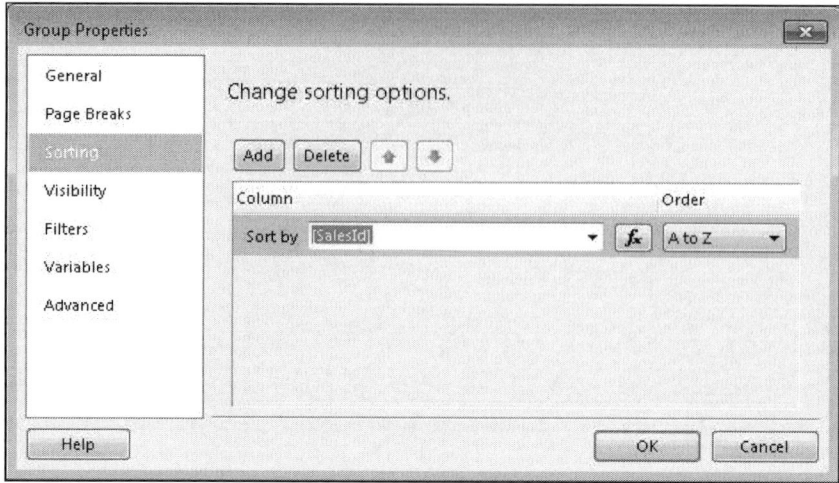

Enable sorting for Sales ID

Adding parameters to control the data displayed in the report

Tom, the Sales manager, also wants an "Order lines not posted" report available under **Accounts Receivable | Reports | Transactions | Sales Orders** to have a parameter to perform a filter on the Sales category.

To add a new parameter to an existing report, perform the following steps:

1. Open Microsoft Visual Studio 2010 from the Start menu.
2. Click on **View | Application Explorer**.
3. Browse for the **SalesNotInvoiced** report under **AOT | SSRS reports | Reports**.
4. Right-click on the report and click on **Edit**.
5. Browse to the report parameters.
6. Right-click on **parameters** and navigate to **Add | Parameter**.
7. Rename the parameter to `SalesNotInvoicedDP_SalesCategory`.
8. Change the Prompt string property to **Sales category**.
9. Right-click on the report design named **Report** and navigate to **Edit using Designer**.

10. Right-click on **Tablix** and select **Properties**.
11. Switch to the **Filters** tab and click on the **Add** button
12. Provide the below values in the filter:

    1. Expression as **[SalesCategory_Name]**.
    2. Operator as **=**.
    3. Value as **Paramters!SalesNotInvoicedDP_SalesCategory.Value**.

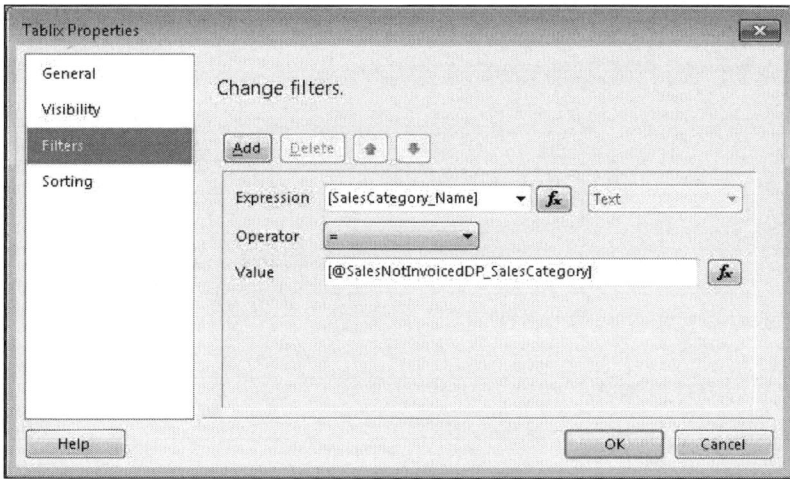

Filters

Summary

In this chapter, we learned how to edit existing reports using Visual Studio, with various methods, deploying reports to the Report Server using various methods, saving reports back to the AOT, and also how to perform specific modifications in an out-of-the-box using a real-time scenario. Furthermore, we will learn about reporting best practices, common SSRS expressions, and common AX reporting classes in the appendices.

Common SSRS Expressions

String functions

A list of common string functions is given in the following table:

No	Function name	Description	Syntax

1	GetChar	This function returns a specific character from the string.	`=GetChar(StringValue, Position)`
			For Example:
			`GetChar("Red",2)`
			Returns:
			`e`

2	InStr	This function returns the starting position of the first occurrence of one string within another.	`=InStr(StringValue1, StringValue2)`
			For Example:
			`InStr("My Car is Red","Car")`
			Returns:
			`4`

3	LCase	This function converts a string to lower case.	`=LCase(StringValue)`
4	UCase	This function converts a string to upper case.	`=UCase(StringValue)`
5	StrReverse	This function reverses the string.	`=StrReverse(StringValue)`

No	Function name	Description	Syntax

6	Mid	This function gets a character from the middle of the string.	`=Mid(StringValue, StartPosition, No of char)`
			For Example:
			`Mid("Car",2,1)`
			Returns:
			`a`

7	Replace	This function replaces a string value with another string value.	`=Replace(StringValue, FindString, ReplaceString)`
8	Space	This function adds spaces.	`=Space(No of spaces)`

A list of common date functions are described in the following table:

No	Function name	Description	Syntax
1	today	This function is used to return today's date.	`=today()`

2	DateAdd	This function is used to add values to the date; we can add the number of days, months, and year. We can use intervals as the following values:
		
		• d: Day
		• m: Month number
		• q: Quarter
		• yyyy: Year
		• h: Hour
		• n: Minutes
		• s: Seconds
			`=DateAdd(DateInterval, Number, DateValue)`
			For Example:
			`=DateAdd("m",1,today())`

3	DateDiff	This function is used to get the difference between two dates. We can get the difference in terms of days, months, years, and so on. Refer to the interval as explained in the `DateAdd` function.	`=DateDiff(DateInterval, DateValue,DateValue)`

No	Function name	Description	Syntax
4	monthName	This function returns the month name.	=monthName(M onthNumber, Abbreviate)
5	WeekdayName	This function returns the name of the weekday. It will generally start as 1 for Sunday, 2 for Monday, and will go up to 7, that is Saturday.	=WeekdayName (DayNumber, Abbreviate)
6	First day of current week	This function returns the first day of the current week.	=DateAdd("d" ,- DatePart("w" ,Today,0,0)+ 1,Today)
7	Last date of month	This function will return the last day of the month.	=DateAdd("d" ,- 1,cdate("3/1 /2013"))
8	DatePart	This function will return a specific value from the date. Refer to the interval as explained in the DateAdd function.	=DatePart(Da teInterval,D ateValue)

A list of common format functions is given in the following table:

No	Function name	Description	Syntax
1	Change color of textbox	This function allows changing the color of the text box based on a value.	For Example: =IIf(Fields!Prof itPercent > 70, Green, Red)
2	Currency	This function converts the real value to a currency.	For Example: =Format(1223321, "C")
3	Number	This function converts the value to a number.	For Example: =Format(1223321, "N1") Returns: 1223321.0

No	Function name	Description	Syntax

4	FormatDateTime	This function converts the date and time format to the required format.	For Example:
			
			`=FormatDateTime(`
			`Date.Value,1)`
			`=FormatDateTime(`
			`Date.Value,2)`
			`=FormatDateTime(`
			`Date.Value,3)`
			`=FormatDateTime(`
			`Date.Value,4)`
			
			Returns:
			
			`Thursday, July`
			`12, 2013`
			`7/12/2013`
			`12:00:00AM`
			`00:00`

5	Format	This function converts a date value to a required format. We can use the following format descriptions for the date:
		
		• dd: Day of month
		• ddd: Day of week (Abbreviate)
		• dddd: Day of week (Full name)
		• MMM: Month name (Abbreviate)
		• MMMM: Month name (Full name)
		• y: Year (Last 1 or 2 digit)
		• yy: Year (Last 2 digit)
		• yyyy: Year
			For Example:
			
			`=Format(Date.Val`
			`ue,"dd-MM-yyyy")`
			
			Returns:
			
			`12-07-2013`

A list of common global functions is described in the following table:

No	Function name	Description	Syntax
1	Execution time	This functions returns the time when the report runs.	=Globals!ExecutionTime
2	Page number	This function returns the current page number.	=Globals!PageNumber
3	Report folder	This function returns the full report path (physical location not Report Server URL).	=Globals!ReportFolder
4	Report name	This function returns the report name.	=Globals!ReportName
5	Report server URL	This function returns the Report Server URL where the report is executed.	=Globals!ReportServerUrl
6	Total pages	This function returns the total pages in the report.	=Globals!TotalPages
7	User Id	This function returns the current User ID who is running the report.	=User!UserID
8	Language	This function returns the current language in which the report is rendered.	=User!Language

B

Common Standard AX Classes and Methods

Common classes and their purpose

The following table lists common classes and their purpose:

No	Class name	Description	Used ideally
1	Report data provider class (RDP) extends to `SRSReportDataProviderBase`	Report data provider class is used to build up datasets and populates values in them using a complex set of business logic.	When data is to be fetched from multiple queries and also includes complex calculations.
2	Report data provider (RDP) contract Use attribute: `[DataContractAttribute]`	RDP contracts are used to provide parameters to the report. On the basis of which, queries get executed during report processing, and fetch data from the database.	When specific parameters are required to filter data in the report.

No	Class name	Description	Used ideally
3	Print contract extends to `SrsPrintDestinationSettings`	Contract which contains all contracts like query contract, print contract, RDP contract, RDL contract once report RDL is parsed.	Not to be overridden.
4	Query contract. No class, instead a map object which contains parameters and a query object.	Contract which provides a query contract to the report.	Not to be overridden.
5	Controller extends to `SrsReportRunController`	The controller for a set of reports having the same functionality. This class controls the behavior of the reports, like on the basis of a caller, which reports to render.	When multiple designs are available for a report or multiple reports are rendered using the same controller.
6	UI Builders extends to `SrsReportDataContractUIBuilder` and `SysOperationAutomaticUIBuilder`	UI Builders are used to provide a layout to various parameters we add using contracts. Also, we can control the behavior of contracts using the UI Builder class.	Proper UI has to be built up or the parameter behavior has to be modified.
7	Preprocess: `SrsReportDataProviderPreProcess`	The `Preprocess` class prepares the data, before the report is rendered to the user in report viewer control.	When dealing with huge data and reports take a long time to run which may lead to time-out issues.

Common methods and their purposes

The following table lists the common classes and their purposes:

No	Method name	Description
1	Process report: `SrsReportDataProviderBase .ProcessReport()`	This method is called by SSRS at runtime which is used to execute the business logic and prepare datasets with appropriate values.
2	Parm data contract: `SrsReportDataProviderBase .parmDataContract()`	This method is used to get or set the data contract for the RDP.
3	E-mail attachment format: `SRSPrintDestinationSettings .emailAttachmentFileFormat()`	This method is used to provide the file format for an email attachment. Use enumeration: `SrsReportFileFormat`
4	E-mail to: `SRSPrintDestinationSettings .emailTo()`	This method is used to provide the ID of the recipient of the mail.
5	Parm report contract: `SrsReportRunController. parmReportContract()`	This method is used to get or set report contracts.
6	Parm report name: `SrsReportRunController. parmReportName()`	This method is used to provide a report name which has to be rendered in report viewer.
7	Parm show dialog: `SrsReportRunController. parmShowDialog()`	This method is used to control the visibility of the report dialog.
8	Pre-prompt modify contract: `SrsReportRunController. prePromptModifyContract()`	This method is used to modify report contract values on the basis of the caller, before the report dialog is prompted.
9	Pre-run modify contract: `SrsReportRunController. preRunModifyContract()`	This method is used to modify report contract values before running the report.

No	Method name	Description

10	Add dialog field:
	`SrsReportDataContractUIBuilder.`
	`addDialogField()`
		This method is used to add dialog fields to the report dialog box.

11	Post run:
	`SrsReportDataContractUIBuilder.`
	`postRun()`
		This method is used to execute post run actions.

12	Parm user connection:
	`SrsReportDataProviderPreProcess.`
	`parmUserConnection()`
		This method is used to get or set a user connection for the report in execution.

C
Reporting Best Practices

Best practices for AX 2012 report development

In this appendix, we will learn about the best practices followed for all reporting objects.

Report table

The following points must be kept in mind while developing reports:

Do's

- While using the `SrsReportDataProviderPreProcess` class as RDP, use the `Regular` table to insert data in the reporting table. Also, set the `CreatedTransactionId` property to `Yes`.

- Use `TempDB` tables when dealing with a large amount of data.

- Use **Extended Data Types (EDT)** for the `temp` table fields so that the labels and other properties would be automatically handled by the report framework when the report is rendered.

- Provide proper labels to the fields, in case EDT is not used for a field.

- Provide proper indexes.

- Provide table relations to the foreign key fields, to enable Auto links to the report. It helps to drill-through to the master form.

Don'ts

- Use the `TempDB` or `InMemory` table as the reporting table while using the `SrsReportDataProviderPreProcess` class as RDP
- Use the `Regular` table when extending to `SrsReportDataProviderBase`

The RDP class

The following points must be kept in mind while developing reports:

Do's

- When dealing with a complex query involving multiple joins, use the RDP class to insert data into the `temp` table and render data onto the report.
- When dealing with a large amount of data, use the `SrsReportDataProviderPreProcess` class.
- Use a user connection at the beginning of the `processReport()` method while using the `SrsReportDataProviderPreProcess` class as RDP.
- Perform database related functions to be executed on the server only.
- Use the `processReport()` method to process business logic. Also, set `SysEntryPointAttribute` at the beginning of `processReport()`.

Don'ts

- Use RDP if a dataset can be generated by a query
- Use client based operations like printing information, warnings, or errors

The Contract class

The following points must be kept in mind while developing reports:

Do's

- Use the `contract` class to add parameters to the report
- Perform a validation to check if all parameters have correct values, or to check the mandate parameters

Don'ts

- Provide labels if they can come from EDT

The Controller class

The following points must be kept in mind while developing reports:

Do's

- While dealing with multiple designs, use the `controller` class
- Use the `controller` class to modify contracts

Don'ts

- Process business logic in the `controller` class
- Send the dataset to the RDP class

The UI Builder class

The following points must be kept in mind while developing reports:

Do's

- Use the UI Builder class when a specific UI is required to be rendered before the report generation.
- Use the `build` method to add all dialog fields to the report dialog.
- Use the `postRun()` method to override dialog fields behavior. For example, providing lookups and modified events

Don'ts

- Modify contracts in the `UI Builder` class
- Control visibility of parameters in the `UI Builder` class

Report design

The following points must be kept in mind while developing reports:

Do's

- Use templates for designing reports to provide a report presentation across the system
- Use labels in Caption and Description properties for report controls
- Use Auto Design for all simple reports
- Use a proper report name, so that it can be easily referred back in AOT

Don'ts

- Use Auto Design for form based reports like Invoice or Confirmation reports, where a field's position has to be set to a value, instead of Auto
- Include a report design in the report which is not used

AOT queries

The following points must be followed while developing reports:

Do's

- Provide a field list while creating a query, so that only required field values are selected
- Provide proper relations when joining data sources

Don'ts

- Use Query directly in a report which has multiple joins and grouping, instead use the RDP class

Index

A

AOT
report project, adding 66
AOT Query
creating 11
dont's 110
do's 110
Application Object Tree query. *See* **AOT query**
Auto Design report
AOT Query, creating 11, 12
creating 14, 15, 16, 18
deploying, to the Report Server 19
executing 20
prerequisites 11
Report Model project, creating 14
saving, to AOT 18
scenario 10
Auto Design report, RDP class used
deploying, to the Report Server 82
executing 82
prerequisites 77
Report data provider class, creating 77, 78
Report Model project, creating 78
saving, to AOT 82
scenario 77
Table report, creating 79, 80
AX 2012 R2
URL, for out-of-box reports 65
AX 2012 report development
best practices 107

B

best practices, AX 2012 report development
AOT queries 110
Contract class 108
Controller class 109
RDP class 108
report design 110
report table 107
The UI Builder class 109

C

Chart control 39
Chart report
AOT Query, creating 45-47
Auto Design SSRS report, creating 48, 49
creating 45
deploying, Microsoft Dynamics AX 2012 Management Shell used 51
deploying, to the Report Server 51
prerequisites 45
Report Model project, creating 48
running 52
saving, to AOT 51
scenario 45
classes
lists 103, 104
Contract class
dont's 109
do's 108
Controller 70

Controller class
  about 69, 70
  activities 70
  dont's 109
  do's 109
  overriding 71

D

DateAdd function 98
DateDiff function 98
date functions
  DateAdd 98
  DateDiff 98
  DatePart 99
  First day of current week 99
  Last date of month 99
  monthName 99
  today 98
  WeekdayName 99
DatePart function 99
Drill-through report
  creating 21
  deploying, to the Report Server 34
  parameter, adding to purchase order
      details report 31
  parameter, adding to purchase order
      list report 30
  prerequisites 21
  Purchase order details report,
      creating 25-27
  Purchase order list report, adding 33
  Purchase order list report, creating 24, 25
  Report Model project, creating 22
  saving, to AOT 34
  scenario 21
  Vendor list report, adding 32
  Vendor list report, creating 22, 23
Dynamics AX Model Projects 64

F

FormatDateTime function 100
Format function 100
format functions
  Change colour of textbox 99

  Currency 99
  Format 100
  FormatDateTime 100
  Number 99

G

Gauge control 39
GetChar function 97
global functions
  Execution time 101
  Language 101
  Page number 101
  Report folder 101
  Report name 101
  Report server URL 101
  Total pages 101
  User Id 101

I

Image control 39
InStr function 97

L

LCase function 97
Line control 38
List control 39

M

Matrix control 39
Matrix report
  creating 40
  creating, Auto Design used 41-43
  deploying, to the Report Server 43
  prerequisites 40
  Report Model project, creating 40
  running 44
  saving, to AOT 43
  scenario 40
methods
  lists 105
Microsoft Dynamics AX 2012
  about 55

reports, creating using external
    data source 55
Microsoft Dynamics AX 2012
    Management Shell
  used, for deploying Chart report 51
Mid function 98
Model 69
monthName function 99
MVC
  about 69
  Controller 70
  Model 69
  View 70

N

native mode 8, 9

P

parameters
  adding, to report 94, 95
Precision Design report
  creating 82
  creating, from Auto Design 82
  deploying, to the Report Server 83
  executing 83
  page break, adding 83
  saving, to AOT 83
  totals, adding to Amount field 82

R

RDL 70
RDP 70
RDP class
  dont's 108
  do's 108
Rectangle control 39
Replace function 98
Report contract class
  about 76
  defining 76
report, creating with external data source
  external report data source, creating 59
  prerequisites 56
  preview 62

report appearances, modifying 61
report data, preparing 56, 57, 58
report project, creating 58
reports, creating 59, 60
scenario 56
Report data provider class
  about 76
  defining 76
  uses 76
report deployment mechanisms
  about 66
  Microsoft Dynamics AX 66
  Microsoft Dynamics AX 2012
    Management Shell 66, 67
  Microsoft Visual Studio 66
report design
  dont's 110
  do's 110
reporting services modes
  about 8
  native mode 8
  SharePoint integrated mode 9
Report Model project, Auto Design report
  creating 14
report project
  adding, to AOT 66
reports, editing in Visual Studio
  changes, deploying to the Report Server 92
  changes, saving to AX 92
  SSRS Report Model Project,
    finding in AOT 90
report table
  dont's 108
  do's 107
report, with parameters
  contract class, creating 84, 85
  creating 84
  deploying, to the Report Server 87
  executing 87
  prerequisites 84
  RDP, modifying 86
  Report Dataset, refreshing 86
  saving, to AOT 87
  scenario 84

S

Sales order ID
  sort order, enabling 93
SharePoint integrated mode 9
Space function 98
SQL Business Intelligence Studio 37
SQL Server Reporting Services. *See* **SSRS**
SrsReportDataContractUIBuilder class 72
SrsReportRunController class 70
SSRS
  about 7
  Auto Design report, creating with AX
        Query 10
  date functions 98
  Drill-through report, creating 21
  format functions 99
  global functions 101
  reporting services modes 8
  string functions 97
string functions
  GetChar 97
  InStr 97
  LCase 97
  Mid 98
  Replace 98
  Space 98
  StrReverse 97
  UCase 97
StrReverse function 97
Subreport control 39
SysOperationAutomaticUIBuilder class 73

T

Table control 38
Textbox control 38
today function 98
tools, advanced reporting 37

U

UCase function 97
The UI Builder class
  about 72
  activities 72

  dont's 109
  do's 109
  SrsReportDataContractUIBuilder class 72
  SysOperationAutomaticUIBuilder class 73
user interface class 69

V

View 70
Visual Studio
  about 63
  advanced reports, creating 37
  reports, editing 90
  tools, advanced reporting 38
Visual Studio Project
  about 63
  reports, adding 65

W

WeekdayName function 99

Thank you for buying
Developing SSRS Reports for Dynamics AX

About Packt Publishing

Packt, pronounced 'packed', published its first book "Mastering phpMyAdmin for Effective MySQL Management" in April 2004 and subsequently continued to specialize in publishing highly focused books on specific technologies and solutions.

Our books and publications share the experiences of your fellow IT professionals in adapting and customizing today's systems, applications, and frameworks. Our solution based books give you the knowledge and power to customize the software and technologies you're using to get the job done. Packt books are more specific and less general than the IT books you have seen in the past. Our unique business model allows us to bring you more focused information, giving you more of what you need to know, and less of what you don't.

Packt is a modern, yet unique publishing company, which focuses on producing quality, cutting-edge books for communities of developers, administrators, and newbies alike. For more information, please visit our website: www.packtpub.com.

About Packt Enterprise

In 2010, Packt launched two new brands, Packt Enterprise and Packt Open Source, in order to continue its focus on specialization. This book is part of the Packt Enterprise brand, home to books published on enterprise software – software created by major vendors, including (but not limited to) IBM, Microsoft and Oracle, often for use in other corporations. Its titles will offer information relevant to a range of users of this software, including administrators, developers, architects, and end users.

Writing for Packt

We welcome all inquiries from people who are interested in authoring. Book proposals should be sent to author@packtpub.com. If your book idea is still at an early stage and you would like to discuss it first before writing a formal book proposal, contact us; one of our commissioning editors will get in touch with you.

We're not just looking for published authors; if you have strong technical skills but no writing experience, our experienced editors can help you develop a writing career, or simply get some additional reward for your expertise.

**Implementing Microsoft Dynamics
AX 2012 with Sure Step 2012**

ISBN: 978-1-84968-704-1   Paperback: 234 pages

Get to grips with AX 2012 and learn a whole host of
tips and tricks to ensure project success

1. Get the confidence to implement AX 2012
   projects effectively using the Sure Step 2012
   Methodology

2. Packed with practical real-world examples as
   well as helpful diagrams and images that make
   learning easier for you

3. Dive deep into AX 2012 to learn key technical
   concepts to implement and manage a project

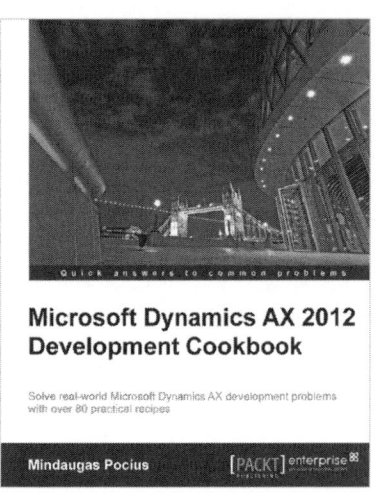

**Microsoft Dynamics AX 2012
Development Cookbook**

ISBN: 978-1-84968-464-4   Paperback: 372 pages

Solve real-world Microsoft Dynamics AX development
problems with over 80 practical receipes

1. Develop powerful, successful Dynamics
   AX projects with efficient X++ code with
   this book and eBook

2. Proven recipes that can be reused in numerous
   successful Dynamics AX projects

3. Covers general ledger, accounts payable,
   accounts receivable, project modules and
   general functionality of Dynamics AX

4 Step-by-step instructions and useful
   screenshots for easy learning

Please check **www.PacktPub.com** for information on our titles

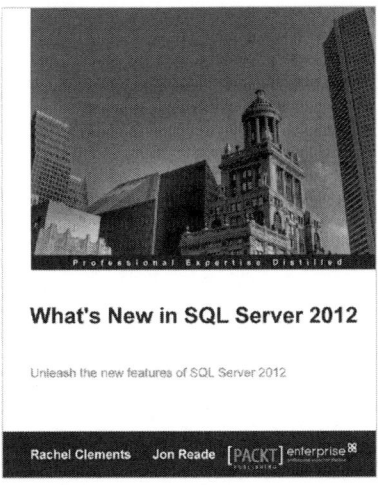

What's New in SQL Server 2012

ISBN: 978-1-84968-734-8   Paperback: 238 pages

Unleash the new features of SQL Server 2012

1. Upgrade your skills to the latest version of SQL Server

2. Discover the new dimensional model in Analysis Services

3. Utilize data alerts and render reports to the latest versions of Excel and Word

4. Build packages to leverage the new features in the Integration Services environment

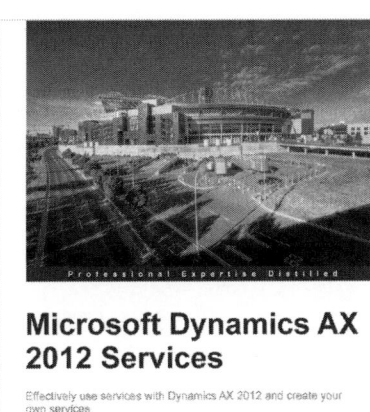

Microsoft Dynamics AX 2012 Services

ISBN: 978-1-84968-754-6   Paperback: 196 pages

Effectively use services with Dynamics AX 2012 and create your own services

1. Learn about the Dynamics AX 2012 service architecture.

2. Create your own services using wizards or X++ code

3. Consume existing web services and services you've created yourself

Please check **www.PacktPub.com** for information on our titles

9143993R00074

Printed in Great Britain
by Amazon.co.uk, Ltd.,
Marston Gate.